Using Informal Education

An alternative to casework, teaching and control?

EDITED BY

Tony Jeffs
and Mark Smith

Open University Press
Milton Keynes · Philadelphia

Open University Press
Celtic Court
22 Ballmoor
Buckingham
MK18 1XW

and
1900 Frost Road, Suite 101
Bristol, PA 19007, USA

First Published 1990

British Library Cataloguing in Publication Data

Using informal education: an alternative to casework, teaching
    and control? – (Innovations in education)
    1. Informal education
    I. Jeffs, Tony, *1943*–   II. Smith Mark, *1950*–   III.
    Series
    371

    ISBN 0 335 09266 7
    ISBN 0 335 09265 9 (pbk)

Library of Congress Cataloging-in-Publication Data

Using informal education: an alternative to casework, teaching,
    and control? / edited by Tony Jeffs and Mark Smith.
        p.   cm. – (Innovations in education)
    Includes bibliographical references.
    ISBN 0-335-09266-7. – ISBN 0-335-09265-9 (pbk.)
    1. Non-formal education.   2. Educational innovations.   I. Jeffs,
Tony.   II. Smith, Mark, 1950 June 25–   III. Series.
LC45.3.U85   1990
374–dc20
                                        89-39424 CIP

Typeset by Rowland Phototypesetting Ltd
Bury St Edmunds, Suffolk

Printed and bound in Great Britain by
Marston Lindsay Ross International Ltd,
Oxfordshire

Contents

Notes on contributors

DON BLACKBURN works at Humberside College of Higher Education.

MAL BLACKBURN works for Humberside Social Services.

DAVID BURLEY is a Community Patch Coordinator, City North, Peterborough. He has also worked in Leicestershire and Gloucestershire, and in the Young Volunteer Resources Unit at the National Youth Bureau as a training and development adviser.

JOHN W. ELLIS is a vicar and youth worker in Grimsby. He studied at Trinity College, Dublin, and was ordained into the Anglican ministry in 1966. He is also qualified as a youth and community worker. Before going to Grimsby he served in Lisburn, Northern Ireland and London.

ANNE FOREMAN is an Assistant Principal Youth and Community Officer for Sutton. She was a centre-based youth worker for five years. Before that she worked for many years as an unqualified worker in social work and community work.

GLYNIS FRANCIS is a curriculum development and training worker with Tameside Metropolitan Borough Council. She has considerable experience of community work and youth work in both the voluntary and statutory sectors and has also worked as a tutor at Manchester Polytechnic.

PAULINE GERTIG is a senior social worker with a team specializing in work with elderly people in Newcastle. She has also worked in a psychogeriatric assessment unit and in an intake team.

TONY JEFFS is a lecturer in the Department of Social Work and Social Policy, Newcastle-upon-Tyne Polytechnic. He was the founding editor of *Youth and Policy* and, with Pam Carter and Mark Smith, edits the *Social Work and Social Welfare Yearbook*.

ELIZABETH AFUA SINCLAIR worked as an actress in various television, radio and stage productions for fifteen years, before training as a youth worker. At present she is employed as a neighbourhood development worker in Brent.

DEBBIE SADDINGTON worked as a community worker with Northumberland Probation Service. She is currently undertaking an MPhil in social work at Newcastle University.

MARK SMITH is a tutor at the Centre for Professional Studies in Informal Education, YMCA National College, London. With Pam Carter and Tony Jeffs he edits the *Social Work and Social Welfare Yearbook*.

Preface

Debates about welfare practice tend to be confined within professional boundaries: teachers exploring group work will often make little reference to the thinking and experience of social workers and their exploration will largely be conditioned by the experience of one particular organizational or institutional form: 'the school'. Yet one of the distinctive, and often neglected, features of the current situation in welfare practice is the extent to which certain forms transcend professional boundaries. Thinking and practice in informal education is one such arena.

We would not want to argue that social work is coming to resemble school teaching or youth work. Nor are we concerned here with looking for some grand underlying theory of welfare intervention. Rather, we want to enhance the practice of informal education by drawing together some key strands from different areas of welfare. This is particularly important in the case of informal education. Within the mainstream of, say, social work or teaching, informal education may be considered somewhat marginal. Yet when the informal educational activities of social workers are joined to those of probation officers, teachers, community workers, youth workers and health workers, we have a significant body of practice and thinking which reveals the possibilities of informal education as a method in welfare work.

Editing books like this is always something of an adventure. Having asserted that informal education is an emerging practice which crosses traditional demarcation lines, there is always the possibility that the contributors will prove you wrong. Thankfully they have not; but the different areas upon which they focus lead to particular insights and orientations. This has made the experience of editing this book particularly pleasing and enjoyable; it was enhanced by the commitment and abilities of the various contributors. To them our thanks.

A number of other people must also be mentioned. The burden of editing books like this falls not only on the editors but on others in their households. As we write these words, Christopher Rogers is asking the question 'Why is it always me?', having interrupted us with a query about his homework. Alex Rogers had asked the same question a few minutes earlier after a request to watch a video had been refused. Andrew Jeffs and Alistair Jeffs must be mentioned if only to be pacified; at least the royalties will provide some compensation in the form of Rick Astley and Kylie Minogue albums. Jackie Apperley and Chris Gibbs, both gifted informal educators, have made a considerable contribution to the book through their readiness to offer a critique of our work. All must be thanked for making space for us and for their help and encouragement. Thanks must also go to Beatrice Michon who processed a couple of the contributions for us and to Colin Fletcher, the series editor, and everybody at Open University Press for their usual efficiency and their support for this project.

Lastly, we would be wanting to express our thanks to Josephine Macalister Brew if she were still alive. She is probably best known for her seminal contributions to youth work thinking (1943, 1957). We are also indebted to her for writing *Informal Education. Adventures and Reflections* (1946), one of the first sustained discussions of informal education outside of schooling.

Tony Jeffs
Mark Smith

CHAPTER 1

Using informal education

TONY JEFFS AND MARK SMITH

Informal education has been an element of practice within casework, schooling, youth work, residential care and the Probation Service for some time. It has been an important part of the activity of community organizations. Yet it has rarely been given sustained attention, though this has changed somewhat in recent years, as the contributors to this book show. Within the criminal justice area, for example, as Debbie Saddington suggests, there has been a shift towards crime prevention and reduction, increased community participation and some form of education which reflects a move from pathological to interactionist perspectives. This has produced an increased readiness in some quarters to look at informal approaches. David Burley argues that the pressure to inject more 'relevance' into secondary school provision has led to a growing interest in informal approaches. Forms of work, complementary to the formal, have emerged which allow teachers to establish different relationships with their students. Within residential work the shift to community care and changes in the way people with severe learning difficulties are viewed has had a similar impact, as Don Blackburn and Mal Blackburn report. Finally, in youth work dissatisfaction with the largely rhetorical notion of social education has led to a reawakening of interest in informal education. With such changes taking place it is important to examine how informal education is actually understood and practised within different arenas and to explore some of the central questions and issues that arise for practitioners.

Informal education and other educational forms

Informal education tends to be defined by its relationship to formal education. While this is important, it is too easy to characterize

informal education negatively as the bit left over. It is better
to identify the positive attributes and compare these with more
formal approaches. This allows us to assess the claims made for the
'improving qualities' of informal education rather than merely
presenting it as a blanket alternative to, say, casework or classroom
work.

In the chapters which follow a number of elements are emphasized. There is the focus on the everyday. On the one hand Don
Blackburn and Mal Blackburn explore the process of dealing with,
and learning from, the apparently trivial tasks of day-to-day living.
On the other, Glynis Francis examines the possibilities of connecting
with fundamental aspects of people's lives. She also stresses the
crucial importance of social relations in informal education. Debbie
Saddington talks about its largely relaxed atmosphere and the way in
which it connects with, and feeds off, other tasks such as those
associated with community groups. Elizabeth Afua Sinclair under-
lines the centrality of addressing and working with the culture of the
learners. Anne Foreman highlights the personality and role of the
practitioner. Both David Burley and Pauline Gertig examine the
way in which informal education may be approached from more
formal contexts. John Ellis brings out the conversational, story-
telling dimension. Above all he, along with the other contributors,
stresses the need to ensure that learning is seen as the responsibility of
the learner. Much of the educator's task is concerned with enabling
people to take that responsibility.

All this indicates that there is something distinctive about informal
education. It is a useful starting point to consider it as a set of ideas
and processes which pay particular attention to, and make use of, the
fabric of daily life. Workers have their professional identity significantly moulded by that fabric. Familiar relationships and institutions
provide much of the material and context for intervention. At the
same time practitioners also draw upon those traditions of thinking
and acting which we define as education. They do so in a way which
allows processes and institutions to develop which make sense in,
and of, the context in which they are applied. These do not necessarily conform to the regular or prescribed forms of the educational
system. One way of catching part of the flavour of the approach is
to describe it as 'using the familiar critically in order to further
learning'.

We can see in this the importance of informal education for
practitioners. At one level there is the potential of informality: the
concern to connect with familiar cultural forms, the flexibility of

response, and the desire to make interventions which make sense in people's lives all hold promise, as the contributors to this book demonstrate. At another level there are the possibilities of education, which are particularly attractive to those practitioners who feel constrained by what they perceive as 'policing' or 'conditioning' forms of practice.

At this point several things need saying. What we are describing here is primarily an approach to educating: a form of pedagogy. As such, informal education emphasizes certain values and concerns: the worth placed on the person of the learner, the importance of critical thinking, and the need to examine the taken for granted. At the same time, informal education need not imply particular content, other than that arising directly from the processes adopted and the values they express. This is an important point to grasp. Informal education is a special set of *processes* which involves the adoption of certain broad ways of thinking and acting so that people can engage with what is going on. It cannot be simplistically defined by a set of curricular aims.

Further, it is not an approach to educating confined to those who define themselves first and foremost as educators. It goes beyond a simple concern with setting or organizational sponsorship. In this we differ from those writers who focus on situations and often use a threefold typology, referring to formal, informal and non-formal settings or environments.

> Formal situations are bureaucratic, non-formal are organised but not necessarily in a bureaucratic environment and informal situations are ones where there are no pre-specified, although there are always covert, procedures of interaction
>
> Jarvis 1987: 70

Here the school and the classroom may be seen as offering the paradigm for a formal setting. Within it people play clear roles within a bureaucratic or 'official' organization. Non-formal education may thus be defined as:

> any organized educational activity outside the established formal system – whether operating separately or as an important feature of some broader activity – that is intended to serve identifiable learning clienteles and learning objectives.
>
> Coombs and Ahmed 1973, quoted in Fordham *et al* 1979: 210–11

Informal situations are defined as occurring in social interaction between family members, friends, acquaintances and so on.

We find this particular focus on, and view of, the setting unhelpful and suspect. It is difficult to see what it adds to our understanding and, indeed, it can confuse (Smith 1988: 127–8). Most definitions of the formal and non-formal appear to apply to professional interventions, to educators sponsored by bureaucratic organizations. However, non-professionals often facilitate learning in both formal and 'non-formal' educational situations. We can also see professionals engaging with informal environments as Jarvis conceives them. It is our contention that the question of sponsorship should be separated from that of setting: we can think of informal and formal settings in which professionalized or non-professionalized interventions may occur.

Giving too much attention to setting may mean we miss the point. Practitioners who are engaged in what they call 'informal education' are largely concerned with processes and interactions: they are interested in the way in which different dimensions combine and connect to make a distinctive form of pedagogy. By focusing on the setting we might not only miss the significance of pedagogy also of the practitioner. There certainly has been a tendency within some discussions of informal primary education, and within youth work, to almost apologize for the interventions that practitioners make. In some way the process is seen as having to be natural and spontaneous. Planned interventions by practitioners are considered something of an aberration, to be apologized for. This is not a view we hold.

Informal education is clearly something different from paying attention to the so-called 'hidden curriculum'. The latter may be taken to mean those things which students learn, 'because of the way in which the work of the school is planned and organized but which are not in themselves overtly included in the planning or even in the consciousness of those responsible for the school arrangements' (Kelly 1982: 8). Such a concept need not be restricted to the school. The organization and planning of residential work, social work, youth work and community work also convey similarly powerful messages. Having recognized this, practitioners may then use the informal education approach in order to create an environment in which certain things enter the 'overt curriculum'. However, they could equally use more formal means.

We must recognize that informal education and community education are often confused. It is difficult to argue a concrete case for differences between the two ideas as community education is a will-o-the-wisp which defies comparative analysis. There are obvious difficulties in attempting to define it (see, for example, Martin 1987; Fletcher 1987; and Clark 1987) and it is often used to include all forms of educational (and many non-educational) intervention. It is pointless to attempt to clarify such rhetoric. However, we do need to note that informal educators have been subject to a number of the same intellectual and political influences as many of those who call themselves community educators. For example, Lovett (1988) singles out the writings of Bernstein, Illich and Freire. Bernstein (1971), he suggests, reinforced the belief that language and culture were major barriers in attracting working class people to education:

> Consequently, more attention was paid to working-class and popular culture. Freire confirmed this approach with his concept of cultural invasion and the importance of using everyday life and experience as cultural material in an educational dialogue about concrete issues and problems, linking reflection and action in a continuing praxis.
>
> Lovett 1988: 145–6

Illich (1973) focused on the de-institutionalization of education. The need was to think anew in terms of learning networks which utilized 'a variety of educational resources, formal and informal, including the skills and talents of people themselves' (Lovett 1988: 146).

We should note the way in which the notion of informality has been used within primary schooling in Britain. As Alexander (1988: 148) has commented:

> Certain words have acquired a peculiar potency in primary educa-tion, and few more so than 'informal'. Never properly defined, yet ever suggestive of ideas and practices which were indisputably right, 'informal' was the flagship of the semantic armada of 1960s Primaryspeak . . . spontaneity, flexibility, naturalness, growth, needs, interests, freedom . . . self-expression, discovery and many more.

Important thinkers can be invoked as contributing to the significance of the informal – Rousseau, Pestalozzi, Froebel and Dewey to name but a few (see, for example, Blyth 1988: 7–24). However, since the 1960s the terms of educational debate have altered somewhat and ideas have had to be reformed or redressed in the rhetoric of the moment. It is now less common to hear informal approaches to primary education being advanced as a blanket alternative to formal ones. When we look at usage within discussions of primary schooling, the most consistent form now appears to be the noun 'informality', rather than the adjective 'informal': instead of informal education, we might examine informality in pedagogy, in curriculum, in organization, in evaluation and in personal style (Blyth 1988). What is being examined is a tendency. This development is helpful. Much that has been described as informal primary education would not fit the definition of informal education advanced here: it would either be seen as formal, but containing significant elements of flexibility and openness, or as an informal interlude in a formal programme (more of this later). More recently, and helpfully, certain strands of what was known as informal primary education, for example, person-centredness and a process-orientation, have been reworked within the organizing notion of the 'organic curriculum' (Hunter and Scheirer 1988).

There is often an automatic assumption that informal education means working with small groups. For practitioners who have been used to individualized interventions or structured large groups such as classes, one of the distinctive experiences of informal education may be the use of group work. This is certainly a key medium but it is not the only one. Practitioners may equally be committed to working with individuals, whether directly or through the production of materials and so on; they may also have to intervene in large formal settings such as public meetings and in complex contexts such as youth clubs.

Characteristics of informal education

A number of elements appear to combine in a distinctive form which can be labelled informal education. Here we want to note seven which are drawn from Smith (1988: 126–33) and are illustrated with reference to material in the rest of this book.

To begin with, we can see that informal education can take place in a variety of physical and social settings: there is no regular or prescribed form. Many locales will be primarily for other, non-educational, purposes. For example, in welfare rights work, people are, first and foremost, concerned with finding a way out of some concrete financial problem. Anne Foreman examines the processes in a youth club where the primary focus may be on the pursuit of leisure activities. However, as David Burley demonstrates, informal education can also take place in contexts associated with schooling, like school clubs, visits and residential trips.

The nature of the setting has an impact upon what can be done – and not just at a physical level. Educators (and participants) need to explore how a setting is experienced and how this influences who takes part and how they function. They also have to appreciate the ways in which the setting may relate to the needs of the 'client group'. These considerations can be seen clearly at work in Glynis Francis's discussion of working with community groups. The classic tension is between the work required by a particular activity, such as planning a play scheme or organizing a handball club, and what the group or individual can learn from the process. The primary task for the group or individual is the achievement of some concrete activity or object, rather than learning. Not only can this lead to frustration on the part of educators, it also requires the making of some fine judgements and sensitive interventions. Educators are not there to hijack what groups are trying to do. Yet their interventions have to be primarily directed towards promoting understanding rather than the success of the particular project in hand.

While much of the learning that occurs may initially appear to be incidental, it is not necessarily accidental. We are concerned here with purposeful and conscious actions. The specific goals may not be clear at any one time either to the educator or to the learner. Yet the process is deliberate, in that the people concerned are seeking to acquire knowledge, skills and/or attitudes, even if the goals are not specific (Brookfield 1983: 15). What educators do is contribute to the development of the context and conditions which allow the desired 'internal' change we know as learning to occur. When we look at much youth work practice, for example, it can be seen that the learning cited as evidence of youth workers' educational activities is often, in fact, accidental: the context for learning is frequently not the focus for intervention. The particular activity involved cannot, therefore, be labelled education.

The timescales involved are likely to be highly variable and are often influenced by the dynamics of the institution(s) in which the work is taking place. Practitioners can become dependent upon a range of factors over which they have little control, such as pub opening hours, or the times when people go to the shops. There are also questions of pace and of the relative open-endedness of much informal practice. As Debbie Saddington comments, the process is often slow, with all sorts of apparent cul-de-sacs and diversions. However, when we examine the scale of what is often attempted, and what it actually means for the lives of those worked with, a feeling of slow progress is hardly surprising. This can be heightened by the lack of access to appropriate means for testing progress. In other words, it is only when someone has to act that the extent of learning becomes clear. If that opportunity does not arise, or if educators are not clear about what they are looking for, then a sense of drift can set in. It is often the case that there is no clear end to the work. One thing can lead to another, as the examples in Anne Foreman's chapter demonstrate.

One aspect of informal education noted by many here is the extent to which participants have control over the content of learning. The term 'negotiated learning' is used several times to describe the process. The idea of a contract between the educator and the participants is also underlined. Don Blackburn and Mal Blackburn suggest that such negotiability should apply to both content and method. However, most contributors go beyond negotiability and suggest that participation must also be voluntary and is often self-generated. This poses a fundamental question. To what extent is it possible to describe a process as informal if participation is forced – as is the case of many in probation day centres, residential settings and schools?

It is possible here to make a distinction between the general requirement, for example, of attending a day centre and participation in different activities. While people may have to be in the centre, they may well have a choice as to whether they take part in certain pursuits. Although those voluntary activities may be conditioned by their context there is at least *some* room for informal practice. This will not be without difficulties, as Blackburn and Blackburn's discussion of the preparing and serving of food in residential settings shows. It may be that residents, perhaps as part of a group decision, have to take a share in these activities. However, being required to help with the cooking is quite separate from any educational work about how residents may feel about this requirement. The acid test is whether people freely choose to engage in such reflection.

With the voluntary nature of informal education goes a 'romantic' view of the relationship between educators and learners. It is without a doubt significant that people can choose whether to engage in the process or not. Similarly, the nature of the relationship may be affected by the fact that much of the activity is mounted 'on the participant's ground' (see below). However, this should not be taken as meaning that power differentials disappear or that the roles of enabler and learner are somehow collapsed into one. The statement 'we are all learners here' may well be true at one, highly generalized, level; but it also confuses the real situation. As we have seen, the primary task of educators is to 'manage' the external conditions that facilitate the internal change called learning (Brookfield 1986: 46). This distinguishes them from the learners, who are primarily concerned with the internal act of learning. Where learners take on educational responsibilities, where they set their own learning goals, locate resources, devise learning strategies and are responsible for evaluating the progress made towards the attainment of those goals, they have become educators: they are engaged in self-education or self-directed education (Brookfield 1986: 47). This may well be a goal for some informal educators. However, confused usage of the word 'learning' should not be allowed to cloud fundamental differences.

Many of the following chapters focus on the dialogical nature of informal education and on the mutual respect involved. It is not simply that informal educators engage in conversations but that they give careful attention to words, the ideas that they express and the actions that follow. 'Dialogue should be considered as a form of action aimed at the transformation of our normal communication patterns combined with continuing reflective evaluation of that action' (Allman 1987: 221). Allman goes on (222) to make a useful distinction between discussion and dialogue.

> Discussion focuses primarily on allowing each person to express or communicate and thus clarify in their own minds *what* they think. By contrast, dialogue involves an exploration of *why* we think what we do and how this thinking has arisen historically.

In other words, it is an invitation to critical thinking: to identify and challenge assumptions and explore and imagine alternatives (Brookfield 1987: 15). Beyond that it is an opening to action. It is here that the scale of the task that many informal educators are engaged in becomes clear. What is involved is often nothing less than transforming perspectives: the process by which people 'come to recognize their cultural induced dependency roles and relationships and the reasons for them and take action to overcome them' (Mezirow 1983: 125). As John Ellis later comments, such a change is necessary to avoid new ideas being colonized by the old viewpoint. A central aspect of dialogue in this respect is an emphasis upon collaborative forms of working. This entails:

> a conscious challenge to and transformation of the relations and rituals of our normal form of group communication, discussion, wherein, though socially gathered, people operate as separate

individuals verbally expressing, sometimes exchanging, what they already know.

Allman 1988: 97

One of the important features of this process is that it is often initiated by an external circumstance or stimulus. 'Only rarely does a change in thinking patterns happen because of a person's self-willed decision to become more critically reflective' (Brookfield 1987: 24). Such events, and the dialogue that is necessary to make sense of them, can be, and often needs to be, handled within formal structures. Yet the location, orientation and relative ability of informal educators to use such events means they have a special contribution to make.

Dialogue is not value-free. It involves a certain view of the world and of women's and men's place within it. As Freire notes (1985: 43), 'All educational practice implies a theoretical stance on the educator's part. This stance in turn implies – sometimes more, sometimes less explicitly – an interpretation of man and the world'. We have to accept, and make a commitment to, the philosophy that infuses this notion. This can be seen at work in the process. The educator focuses upon the thinking and actions of the other person. The task is to enable that other to make sense and build theory. This is not done by trying to impose a way of thinking but by asking questions and making statements which enable the other to clarify and problematize his or her own thinking. The same process will often occur when working in groups where there can be a group focus on one individual's thought and action, with the other group members working to help that person clarify and refine his or her understanding. In so doing they also enhance their own learning and enlarge their abilities to participate in dialogue. At other times educators will be alone in the group in their concern to clarify and problematize the thinking of another.

A respect for persons is a precondition for productive dialogue: degrading circumstances and treatment must be opposed. 'The snobbery and patronizing attitudes of the privileged, and the feelings of deference which they foster – the status hierarchy by which people are appreciated not for their personal qualities but for their social position' (Baker 1987: 4) must also be rejected. A respect for truth and for justice, a commitment to collaborative working and a belief in reflectiveness and theory making are all necessary. Crucially, this last belief must connect with action: there has to be some promise of the dialogue resulting in changed or better informed behaviour.

Informal educators must have an active appreciation of, and engagement with, the social systems through which people operate and the cultural forms they use. As Brew put it 'one should use the language of the people' (1946: 40). Rather than creating an institution largely separated from, or beyond the day-to-day context in which people operate, informal educators will attempt to work with or within forms and structures familiar to, and owned by, the participants (Smith 1988: 130). Debbie Saddington, Anne Foreman and John Ellis, for example, look at clubs as sites for informal education and Don Blackburn and Mal Blackburn examine some of the daily rhythms of residential life. One of the important features of this process is that educators pay careful attention to the way in which notions of informality are understood by the people they work with. A particular educator's understanding of 'informality', may not be shared by other participants. A concern for staying with the developing understandings of the participants is central to informal education and this can take on a particular meaning where practitioners are operating across class, ethnic and gender divides.

The identity of informal educators is bound up with a commitment to a dialogue with the social systems and cultures through which learners operate. This involves constantly looking for the learning which can be generated within everyday life. The result can be an enhanced appreciation of the main areas of 'need', the generation of more relevant educational forms and the possibility of better informed work, as John Ellis suggests. It should also allow an awareness of crucial political and cultural questions such as those raised by Elizabeth Afua Sinclair. Above all, it should give a measure of protection against the cultural imperialism of some forms of education. The whole purpose of informal education is to develop forms of thinking and acting that fit the situations that people find themselves in. In the end this can only be done by the participants, which makes *their* analysis and view of the world a central reference point.

Lastly, and contrary to much received opinion, informal education is not only concerned with the pattern of learning usually known as 'experiential'. There is a sense, as Dewey suggests, in which all genuine learning comes about through experience. However, that 'does not mean that all experiences are genuinely or equally educational. Experience and education cannot be directly equated to each other' (1938: 25). Problems appear as soon as we begin to ask what we mean by 'experience'. Some writers have tended to use experience in a concrete rather than cognitive sense. As a result it is possible to argue that there are at least two broad, but separate, patterns of learning: the experiential and the information-assimilational (see, for example, Coleman 1976). The classic expression of the former is Kolb's learning cycle. This begins with concrete experience, proceeds to observation and reflection, then to generalization and abstract conceptualization, then to active experimentation which in turn produces concrete experience. The whole cycle then repeats itself (Kolb 1976). This circular process can then be compared with the supposedly linear process of information assimilation. This begins with the educator transmitting information through some symbolic medium such as a lecture. Some of that information is then received by the learner, assimilated, organized, made into a general principle, applied and action taken. These patterns, as outlined, have different strengths and weaknesses. One pattern may be more usefully applied to a particular situation than the other (Coleman 1976).

 Informal education may, as Glynis Francis and Anne Foreman suggest, put people's experiences at the centre. It may also be person-centred. However, this does not mean that informal educators forego information giving as a technique. In fact, in a number of the accounts that follow (see, for example, Gertig) we see informal educators at certain points offering information rather than attending to concrete experiences. A community worker working with a tenants' group may be asked to provide information about the local authority or about, say, the Housing Action Trust programme. This assists and informs dialogue.

We may conclude that informal educators are not tied to the use of one pattern or style of learning. The adoption by some of so called 'experiential learning' as a central element is perhaps best seen as an aspect of informal educators' search for a professional identity. This parallels the eagerness of some adult educators to construct an empirically verifiable theory of adult learning.

> If we could discover certain empirically verifiable differences in learning styles between children (as a generic category) and adults (as a generic category), then we could lay claim to a substantive area for research that would be unchallengeably the property of educators and trainers of adults. Such a claim would provide us with a professional identity. It would ease the sense of insecurity and defensiveness that frequently assails educators and trainers of adults in all settings when faced with the accusation that they are practising a non-discipline . . . Such a revelation is unlikely to

transpire for some considerable time, and it may be that the most empirically attestable claim that can be made on behalf of adult learning styles concerns their range and diversity.

Brookfield 1986: 33

Informal educators who fail to be sensitive to the possible range of learning styles are also likely to be paying insufficient attention to the cultures with which they are working.

The formal and the informal

Some contrasts with formal education are clear. Formal education will tend to take place in a 'sole-use' setting; have a more explicit and codified curriculum; show different forms of time structuring; participation may or may not be voluntary; processes may or may not be dialogical; and there may not be an active appreciation of people's cultures and social networks (Smith 1988: 132). The institutions and practices associated with the paradigms of organization – the school, college and classroom – will tend to mould the identity of formal educators. However, as Ellis demonstrates, there are marked pitfalls to thinking of informal and formal education as mutually exclusive. They are more akin to traditions of thinking: a programme of informal work may well have formal interludes and the formal programme may gradually change its character. The latter is clearly shown in the work Pauline Gertig describes in relation to carers. The former can be seen where, for example, the practitioner works with individuals in order that they may reflect upon their experiences and begin to build theories. Similarly, formal programmes, as Elizabeth Afua Sinclair shows, can be structured so as to encourage the development of informal learning networks and contain within them a parallel concern to enable dialogue.

It is in this area that the limits of purely informal approaches become clear. Where people are seeking to make sense of their experiences and insights it is quite likely that more formal means will be needed. As John Ellis points out, informal approaches have their shortcomings for dealing with complex questions. Earlier we used the example of the group which focuses upon the learning of one member. That group has to work out and agree certain rules and procedures in order to function. Those sessions where the group consciously uses these 'rules' are to some extent formalized. They may entail some explicit agreements concerning objectives, setting and procedures. It is in this sense that we have talked of informal education having formal interludes.

Educators can find that as soon as they appear the situation alters and the group or individual starts functioning in a different mode. Some practitioners, uncomfortable with the sporadic and 'unfinished' nature of informal work, seek comfort in order and activity; their intervention, perhaps unconsciously, is directed at formalizing the informal. At certain times formalization is appropriate. There will be periods when educators will be involved in more structured work with groups and individuals. As needs change so will the form of intervention. Indeed, it may no longer be appropriate for informal educators to devote much time to working with certain people. Workers commonly find themselves, as Glynis Francis comments, helping people to identify or construct courses and study programmes that meet their own learning needs – A process sometimes described as 'hatching and despatching'. Whether we define an activity as formal or informal is largely a question of balance and time. For work to remain informal the formal was to remain an 'interlude'.

The movement between the formal and informal may not simply take place within education: it may for example, be a movement from education to more structured forms of casework. The social worker may choose to use different forms of intervention in order to approach varying areas of concern. The central point here is that if practitioners operate in only one mode they are likely to be less than effective. There is a need to examine the process of blending the informal and formal and to pay attention to the means by which practitioners switch between modes. This creates many problems.

The problem of curricula

We have already noted that a detailed curriculum is one of the things that demarcates formal from informal education. At the same time a number of schemes have sought to introduce curriculum elements into informal practice often in order to control it. David Burley notes the use of informal education within schools in connection with the profiling of students. Within youth work, as Anne Foreman remarks, there has been a growing emphasis on curriculum by key agencies such as the National Youth Bureau and HM Inspectorate. Don Blackburn and Mal Blackburn discuss the use of Individual Programme Plans (IPPs) by some residential agencies. The central question here is the extent to which the introduction of curriculum thinking alters the educational form. There are dangers in inserting a notion formed in one context into another.

The IPP approach is a useful example of what can happen. It has often included an assessment framework, based upon behavioural objectives. As Blackburn and Blackburn comment, although people with learning difficulties may be involved in a choice of goals when constructing an IPP, the choice is effectively limited by the menu of skills provided in the assessment. A strong focus on curriculum content can easily lead to a type of prescription that undercuts the opportunity for dialogue. The same problem faces those informal educators who, while not having a thorough set of curriculum objectives, do have a specific remit: They may be sent out with, say, a brief to tackle alcohol abuse among young people. The expectations of their managers may conflict with the fact that their interactions with young people are not easily contained within the suggested framework. Pauline Gertig shows how practitioners with precisely detailed objectives often move away from these as their relationship with a group or individual deepens. In other words, there is a shift in emphasis from the objectives of educators, to participants' concerns and interests: a sign that dialogue is possibly occurring.

The adoption of curriculum thinking by some informal educators appears to have largely arisen from a desire to be clear about content. Yet there are crucial difficulties with the notion of curriculum in this context (Smith 1988: 136–9). These centre around the extent to which it is possible to have a clear idea, in advance (and even during the process), of the activities and topics that a particular piece of work will include. At any one time, outcomes may not be highly specific; similarly, the nature of the activities to be used often cannot be predicted. We may be able to say something about how the informal educator will work. However, knowing in advance about broad processes and ethos is not the same as having a knowledge of the programme. We must therefore conclude that approaches to the curriculum which focus on objectives and detailed programmes cannot be accommodated within informal education.

Against such 'curriculum as product' approaches may be set those which focus on process. Stenhouse defines a curriculum as an 'attempt to communicate the essential principles and features of an educational proposal in such a form that it is open to critical scrutiny and capable of effective translation into practice' (1975: 4). Involving both content and method, at a minimum it should 'provide a basis for planning a course, studying it empirically and considering the grounds of its justification' (ibid: 5). Such approaches put deliberation, judgement and meaning making at the centre. They:

place the emphasis upon action or practice, rather than upon some product. Furthermore a practical interest initiates the sort of action which is taken as a consequence of deliberation and a striving to understand or make meaning of the situation on the part of the practitioner rather than action taken as a consequence of a directive or in keeping with some pre-specified objective.

Grundy 1987: 65

While there are still problems regarding prescription many of the elements discussed under the heading of curriculum by those interested in process and practice resonate with the concerns of informal educators. Yet this is to extend the domain of the curriculum. As Barrow comments, there are problems with this. 'By this stage the field of curriculum has become enormous. In fact it is more or less coextensive with the domain of educational studies, of which it is usually presumed to be an offshoot' (Barrow 1984: 6). If we take a fairly narrow definition of curriculum then it quickly becomes clear that it cannot accommodate the sort of ideas and processes discussed in this book. For example, Barrow defines a curriculum as 'a programme of activities (by teachers and pupils) designed so that pupils will attain so far as possible certain educational and other schooling ends or objectives' (1984: 11). It is this understanding of curriculum which broadly informs many of the attempts to introduce the concept into the work of informal educators. Such a product orientation is incompatible with our model.

On the other hand major problems remain if we take a broader understanding of curriculum, even setting aside the conceptual difficulties in extending usage. Many of those investigating process-orientated curricula are doing so in a particular context – that of the formal educational institution. Concepts like 'course' remain central to their model. For example, in discussing their concept of the 'organic curriculum', Hunter and Scheirer describe it as (1988: 95):

a multifaceted, multilevel amalgam of process, subject, problem (or issue) and experience made available to the children . . . The school will have a list of objectives which, while remaining flexible to match the differing needs of individuals, will help the teachers in arriving at appropriate expectations of children's achievements.

Again, we can see here ideas which are alien to the sort of informal education discussed in this book. Informal educational processes do not sit happily with notions such as 'subject'. The objectives of informal educators are more to do with the *delivery* of a service rather than outcomes for individuals. While it is still possible to talk of learning objectives such objectives are the property of the learner rather than the educator. The more detailed such objectives become the more likely it will be that formal forms of intervention are required.

It seems probable that the application of the term 'curriculum' marks off the formal from the informal educator. This is not a conclusion that all our contributors would agree with. Anne Foreman still uses the concept. However, it should be noted that many of the activities she discusses in relation to the 'youth work curriculum' are in fact formal. She also makes use of the idea of 'programme', a notion which has a long history of usage within youth work and which, when used with caution, could be used alongside process-orientated work. However, those wanting to bring meaning-making and process fully into focus have to look for other words to describe their thinking and practice.

Content, direction and process

John Ellis argues that an all-embracing vagueness will not do. There is a deep need for practitioners to be clear on purpose, on the reason why something is done, created or exists. Many of the writers here talk about the direction of specific pieces of work. Such thinking is necessary for making decisions about practice. The idea of *direction* is a useful starting point. It is far broader than the idea of curriculum objectives and carries with it the possibility that the specific topic for study and reflection may vary. Looked at in more detail, we can see that this involves having a personal but shared idea of the 'good': some notion of what makes for human flourishing or well-being (see Brown 1986: 130–63). In other words, our orientation as educators will be informed by having what Dewey describes as an intelligent sense of human interests (1916: 230).

The second element of direction is a disposition towards 'good' rather than 'correct' action. This frame of mind:

> would encourage a person acting in a certain situation to break a rule or convention if he/she judged that to act in accordance with it would not promote 'the good', either generally, or of the person involved in specific situations.
>
> Grundy 1987: 62

At this point we can see a number of ideas coalescing. Informal educators have to 'think on their feet'. Not having predefined learning objectives they reason their way through to what might be appropriate. They are guided in this by their understanding of what makes for the 'good', and a disposition towards good rather than correct action. They can draw upon a repertoire of experiences, theories and ideas to help them make sense of what is happening. In this way they engage in dialogue.

Such dialogue takes place in specific circumstances which will also affect what is happening. The social workers in Pauline Gertig's chapter will be known to have some expertise concerning dementia, carers and the resources available to them. The people they are working with have an interest in that expertise. They also have a wealth of experience and knowledge of their own to contribute. We can see how the dialogue that occurs is likely to be orientated towards particular areas. Out of this interaction, action is generated. However, this is not action for action's sake. It is activity based on a thorough understanding of the situation. From this it can be seen that a necessary element in informal educators' practice is the encourage- ment and enabling of people to think critically about the situations that face them so that they may take action. Informal educators do not appear with a list of curriculum objectives: the areas for learning arise out of dialogue, the direction being shaped by the situation, an evolving reading of what makes for the good and a disposition towards it. To this must also be added the educator's interest in critical thinking and action. This process is summarized in *Figure 1.1*; the different elements are discussed at greater length in Chapter 10.

We can see how the notion of direction fits into the dialogical process. Much of the work described in the following chapters is aimed at encouraging and developing critical thinking and the disposition and ability to act. This is further infused by a concern to develop a fully social understanding. To quote Freire again (1972: 58):

> The pursuit of full humanity . . . cannot be carried out in isolation or in individualism, but only in fellowship and solidarity . . . No one can be authentically human while he prevents others from being so.

These purposes may well be mediated through specific concerns. Nevertheless, the central question that underpins the purpose of any informal education in respect of welfare rights, caring or any of the examples explored here, is to what extent practitioners' interven- tions are directed towards critical reflectiveness and action. To be effective, educators must remain informed by an understanding of

Informal educators enter

> particular
> social and cultural
> situations

with

> personal but
> shared ideas of the
> good

> an ability to think critically,
> and reflect-in-action

> a disposition to
> choose the 'good' rather
> than the 'correct'

> a repertoire of examples,
> images, understandings and
> actions and

> an understanding of
> their identity and role

They encourage

> dialogue
> between, and with,
> people in the situation

out of which may come

> thinking and action

This affects

> those situations,
> the individuals concerned,
> significant others
> and the educators themselves

Figure 1.1   Elements of the informal education process

the direction of their work and how this may have been amended by their dialogue with learners. It is similarly vital that participants reflect upon and clarify what they want from the enterprise and what they have gained.

This leads us on to the question of evaluation. As Grundy and others have argued in respect of process-based approaches to the curriculum, evaluation is an integral and not a separate part of the whole educative process. The central principle underlying evaluation in much that is written about the process within welfare (see, for example, Feek 1988) is the need to make an assessment of how closely the product matches the objectives in the guiding plan. It is the product which is the focus of evaluation. In the case of informal education, evaluation means 'making judgments about the extent to which the processes and practices undertaken through the learning experience furthered the "good" of all participants' (Grundy 1987: 77). In other words, the focus is on the process, how people experience it and what is revealed. This requires the construction of rather different criteria or indicators of success. A key area here is the nature of the dialogue that occurred and, as might be expected, the extent to which the discourse was critical.

Identity, personality and role

A major problem practitioners have with informal education is to do with their professional sense of themselves. For a social worker to operate in this way may entail switching from a casework orientation to an educational one. This can involve a substantial jump in terms of the 'statutory' basis of the work and in the circumstances under which a social worker works. As Hudson comments in respect of work with young women (1984: 48):

> For teachers, their contact with teenagers is organised on the basis of their age rather than gender for most of the time, and their aim is to facilitate age-appropriate cognitive development in large numbers of young people . . . Social workers, on the other hand, are orientated to the help of the individual in trouble. Their contact is with young people who are distinguished by their differences from the normal . . . the ethos of social work is to individuate in the treatment of clients.

While this may be a somewhat simplistic representation of the different modes of thinking, we must recognize that the broad body of knowledge underpinning each profession is different (for example, developmental psychology as against psychoanalytical theory and abnormal psychology). Difficulties occur either in the process of switching, or failing to switch, from one mode to the other. Thus, for example, probation officers may approach their informal educational activities with a frame of reference which seriously undermines the enterprise, or teachers may bring in too much of the classroom, priests too much of the church, and youth workers too much activity organization. This slippage is understandable. In asking practitioners to function across practice areas we are demanding a sophisticated ability to handle and contain divergent ways of thinking. The location of much informal work at the periphery of, for example, teaching and casework, has meant that such thinking and practice has not often played a significant role in sustaining the identity of practitioners in those areas. Even where the worker is primarily engaged in informal education, as is the case with many community workers and youth workers, there are problems. Although there are long traditions of informal practice in these areas not much attention has been given to constructing theory around such educational interventions: one key plank in practitioners' identity is ill-formed. Effective practice is dependent on practitioners paying attention to the way they understand and name their craft.

Both Anne Foreman and Debbie Saddington draw attention to the significance of the practitioner's personality in the nature of the work. In part this reflects their pattern of interests. Workers will find it easier to respond to concerns and questions about which they themselves are also curious. Given the relative freedom that many informal educators enjoy in their work, there are dangers here. It becomes possible for workers to follow their own individual interests rather than those collectively determined or expressed by the learners. Other dimensions such as educators' class, ethnicity, gender and physical make up are also important in the way other people may perceive them, as are disposition and values. How many times have we heard comments about practitioners being 'miserable bastards' or 'nice people who really listen'. We have to recognize that the dialogical and intimate nature of informal education focuses attention on the person of the practitioner: certain personal characteristics are required. These include the ability to handle the unfinished nature of practice in this area and to go at a pace defined by the others; and the readiness to allow people to take responsibility for their own learning and lives. There is also a further, structural, pressure at work here. Informal educators frequently have to work on their own, outside institutions which carry powerful professional character stereotypes: many cannot, unlike teachers in schools, draw on certain stock figures to help establish their authority. Attention is therefore focused even more strongly upon their personality.

We have to recognize that the role we are able to take as informal educators is not only dependent upon what we want it to be but also upon what others allow it to be. A number of factors come into play here. There is the degree of autonomy allowed practitioners by their employers and their colleagues and the way they are viewed. On the whole, informal educators have a degree of discretion as to how they practise and with whom. They may be considered as operating within 'front-line' organizations. Tasks are initiated at the front-line level. For example, it could be argued that social workers 'do not think of casework practice as the application of general departmental rules' (Smith 1979: 35). That position may have changed in the last ten years but some room for manoeuvre remains. Generally there are also major obstacles to the direct supervision of most informal educators' activities. Of course, there are exceptions to this, particularly where the actions of the educator affect colleagues. This can arise within schools, where, for instance, other staff may feel their relationship with students is somehow being compromised by the informality and use of first names that occurs within, say, the youth wing. The question of status also comes into play. Informal educators are often employed within sectors that are non-statutory or possess a low status with 'mainstream' practitioners. Youth workers operating within a school or residential workers in the social services are often looked down upon or deemed 'less important'. This is bound to have implications for the way in which any specialism they may have in informal education is viewed.

Beyond this there are also questions regarding the nature of the sponsoring agency and the direction of its practice. To what extent is it possible to locate work with a collective and collaborative ethos within an agency organized around individualized intervention? The tensions discussed in relation to practitioners' identities can also arise at an organizational level. A lack of appreciation by managers of the timescales involved, the resources necessary and the character of informal work can lead to unrealistic expectations. All this can become reflected in poor job specifications, peculiar organizational structures and inappropriate management, as Burley suggests.

We must consider the way in which practitioners are viewed by the people they are attempting to work with. The question of personality has already been discussed. Overlaying and influencing this are people's perceptions of the employing or sponsoring organization. Informal educators employed by social service departments in order to work with groups of parents whose children are on the 'at risk' register may well be viewed differently from generic neighbourhood workers employed by local community organizations. There is the possibility, as Burley notes, of some forms of informal education being used or seen as punitive and control mechanisms.

It is critical that the educator is seen as an educator. Here it is necessary for practitioners to be open about their work and to explain what they do. They may take time to do this. If a group or individual does not accept this it will be difficult for the educator to function. For example, community workers may be seen as people who give out, or influence the giving out, of grants. If they then attempt to help a group focus on how it is working their intervention may be unwelcome. The educator's understanding of what it is to be an educator is often formed in one culture while the understanding of what is to work with an educator is often formed in another. In the same way misunderstandings can easily arise about the precise meaning of formality and informality.

In conclusion

The characteristics and themes developed in this opening chapter can be seen at work in the contributions that follow. What they demonstrate is that informal education is a vibrant and somewhat undervalued form of practice. One of its significant features is the way in which it transcends professional boundaries. If it is to be fully utilized and developed then action will be required within and across the separate professional areas. This has a number of implications for training. As Don Blackburn and Mal Blackburn ask, how do you train or learn to be an informal educator? What we hope this book will make clear is the potential of informal education as a method in welfare work.

CHAPTER 2

Personality and curriculum

ANNE FOREMAN

We see the Youth Service as deeply educational, in the sense that it should be helping young people become whatever it is in them to be.

HMSO 1982: 15

This affirmation of youth work as an educational process belies its image among other agencies involved with young people. The popular view of youth work as providing leisure activities to keep youngsters out of trouble, and of youth workers as quasi-social workers with a dash of outward bound instructor thrown in, sits uneasily alongside the images of other practioners engaged in informal education. This uneasy position, peripheral to other kinds of informal education, is inappropriate for a service whose prime aim is the personal development of the individual. Such an aim has learning at its core.

On the education stage, the spotlight has centred of late on curriculum: negotiated, development, core, et al. The ambivalence of some youth workers towards the term curriculum, and the lack of an agreed acceptable alternative, has kept youth work in the wings. Such a position, while it may reflect a healthy resistance on the part of youth workers to either aggrandizing or misrepresenting their work, also supports the cause of those who wish to see youth work as leisure or recreation rather than education. It may appear tempting in terms of resources to be outside education, but unless educational criteria are used to evaluate youth work the Youth Service will be on the periphery of leisure provision as well.

Assisting in the personal development of people and enabling them to become critical members of society is for many the *raison d'être* of youth work. To achieve such an aim more definite objectives must be formulated. It is these objectives which many would argue form the 'curriculum' in the Youth Service. A large number of youth workers describe such a set of objectives as a 'programme' rather than as a 'curriculum'. Others use the term 'social education'.

Terminology apart, the Youth Service has a range of activities and processes designed to offer learning opportunities to young people. However, the quality of its informal education provision is uneven. In part this is because of variations in practice, a practice that has developed largely around vague notions of young people's needs. It is also partly because of the relationship between the personality of the youth worker, the concept of the informal educator and the youth work task. The construction and implementation of the curriculum or programme is strongly influenced by the nature of this relationship; yet it has received scant attention from trainers, workers or managers.

It is not simply my personal view that youth work offers an uneven range of informal education provision. The National Advisory Council for the Youth Service (NACYS) has produced a plethora of consultation papers. They have considered a range of curriculum matters, from rural youth work (NACYS 1988d) to the participation of young people in the Youth Service (NACYS 1988a; 1988b; 1988c); from work with unemployed youth (NACYS 1987a) to work with girls and young women (NACYS 1989). Such attention to practice has revealed nuggets of excellence among the ordinary or mediocre. One tangible result of such imbalance is a service strong on identifying the issues affecting young people but less adept at tackling them.

Other factors influence the nature of informal education in the Youth Service. Social and political climates, together with changing views and understanding of the nature of adolescence, have influenced formulations of the youth work task. Indeed, the Youth Service, like other agencies involved with young people, has been carried along with the tide of prevailing views of adolescence; such views have helped determine the style of youth work practice, its content and the allocation of resources.

Youth work practice in the formative years of the Service centred around 'improvement' of young people. Youth workers at the time attempted to create an environment where young people were exposed to socially educative experiences that went beyond the socialization processes of family and working life.'[P]ractice . . .

was designed to change the attitudes, "improve" the culture, and thus modify the behaviour of anyone that it was thought would benefit from it' (Booton 1985: 7). Concern for social order, and a need to improve the standard of health of the population, were factors influencing the direction of practice. The result was a programme of character-building physical activities through which young people were to be helped to become healthy, law-abiding citizens. The development of a statutory service, located within local education authorities, served to consolidate this style of youth work practice and ensured that it lasted well into the 1960s.

The Albermarle Report (HMSO 1960) had an important impact on the youth work curriculum of the 1960s and 1970s. One of the tangible consequences of the report was the injection of some £40 million into the Youth Service. These funds resulted in purpose-built youth centres. Large sports halls, coffee bars, social areas and art and craft rooms ensured that a curriculum was constructed around the learning opportunities such building design afforded. But though the range of activities expanded, the personal development of young people was still largely concerned with the transition from school to working life. It was suggested (Davies 1979; 1986) that the interpretation of social education at this time was a product of the 'never had it so good era' – a time when continued economic growth was assured and the only difficulties facing the young were how to make the most of the new opportunities. The informal education of young people was concerned with individual fulfilment and adjusting to the adult status that came with full-time employment.

By the late 1970s, however, a very different picture had emerged. The economic crisis resulted in cutbacks and restrictions in what was being done with and for young people. Lack of employment opportunities, the changing face of leisure in relation to work and a changing welfare benefits system put economic independence out of reach of large numbers of young people. Day-time youth provision attempted to cater for those without paid employment. Such provision ranged from a social and life-skills training approach, information/advice giving and specialist counselling, to drop in leisure and 'soup kitchen' type facilities.

Curriculum – the youth work approach

Before we explore the relation between curriculum and personality some clarification of the youth work curriculum is required. Youth work is primarily concerned with the personal development of young people. Such development is enhanced by an environment that encourages and enables participation in learning opportunities. These opportunities take the form of a programme of educational activities that provide the basis of curriculum content. The youth work curriculum is, however, more than the programme or practice: it includes everything that enhances learning. The design and layout of a building, its resources and accessibility, the personality of the workers, the times of opening and charges: these are all curriculum matters.

What, then, are the characteristics of good informal education in youth work? Can the relationship between personality and curriculum be altered to strengthen curriculum content?

Youth work practice invokes both formal and informal education. Social workers, adult education tutors and trainers all work in a variety of ways that respond to the experiences of young people. Youth work does not simply acknowledge the experience of young people, however: it starts from *how* young people experience the world. In youth work, 'learning begins with what immediately confronts the learner' (Rosseter 1987: 53). It is this stance of working with how young people experience the world that underpins the youth work curriculum.

The wide range of organizations that make up the Youth Service include autonomous groups with their own aims, such as the Guides and Scouts. The curriculum of such groups is directly related to their declared aims. The youth work curriculum described here belongs to that network of clubs, centres and services provided for young people by local authorities. Involvement in the Youth Service should offer young people the sort of learning opportunities afforded by access to such activities as art, drama, sport, music, health education, decision making, residential experiences, political education, community action and adventure education.

Such activities and concepts have much in common with those of other educators located within Social Services, Adult Education, the Careers Service and other training agencies. There will, for example, be both planned and unplanned learning outcomes and a dialectical relationship between method and content. The planned learning outcomes will be those skills or abilities that increase through participation in the curriculum. The unplanned learning outcomes are more likely to differ in their emphasis. One of the planned learning outcomes of 'Upholstery for beginners', for example, might be the ability to re-cover a chair seat; an increase in personal

confidence or the making of new friends might be unplanned
outcomes. Nevertheless, the curriculum of 'Upholstery for beginners' will be directed towards the acquisition of specific skills and the
interventions used by the educator to increase those skills will shape
the methodology. The youth work curriculum differs only in that it
reverses this order. It cannot pre-plan such interventions, but it has
to create situations where learning can occur. The planned learning
outcomes for the young people involved in improving their music
skills, for example, may be to increase the ability to cooperate with
others and foster decision-making skills. These, rather than improved musical ability (though it may provide a springboard for
this), are where the emphasis lies. The youth work curriculum,
therefore, like those in which other informal educators are involved,
demands a high degree of skill in enabling young people to reflect on
their experience and learn to develop their own capacities.

Youth work and experiential learning

Young people become involved in the Youth Service because they
choose to, and the curriculum is influenced by their experience of the
world. Other agencies involved in informal education use the 'learning by doing' process known as experiential learning. This process
encourages the learners to think about what it is they are learning. It
requires them to be active rather than passive recipients of information or instruction. Some form of activity is used as a vehicle
for learning and the immediate life experiences of the learner are
acknowledged and utilized. Reflection upon what has taken place is
the element in the process that facilitates learning. '[I]t is through . . .
reflection that young people learn about their capacities and responsibilities and how to evaluate their circumstances' (DES 1987a: 5).
The educator's knowledge of the learner's situation contributes to
the content of the the process. Class, race, gender and environmental
questions are considered within the context of the educator's perception of such issues. The experiential learning process takes account of
how such issues affect the daily lives of young people. Effective
youth workers have to be able to understand and use the immediate
and individual experience of young people, while retaining an
overall sense of direction and purpose.

The cult of the 'character'

Youth work practice has been determined by, and has reflected,
prevailing social and political trends and attitudes. The needs of

young people have been, and to a large extent still are, identified by
adults with a concern for social order. As has been described earlier,
the Service received, post-Albemarle, a considerable injection of
funds. The fruits of this legacy can be observed in the numbers of
purpose-built centres, with their coffee bars, sports halls and social
areas, dotted around the country. The maintenance and adminis-
tration of such buildings is absorbing more and more of the time and
energy of youth workers, as is the question of how to adapt such
buildings to contemporary requirements. This is a task that requires
no small degree of ingenuity, imagination and creativity. The
post-Albermarle years also saw an increase in the number of training
courses designed to 'professionalize' the service. What remains of
this legacy?

'Youth Club Workers were not like other adults' (DES 1983: 40)
according to one survey of young people's views. This notion of
appearing 'different' because of their work with young people will
be familiar to other welfare workers and caring agencies. In youth
work it can be linked to the use of activities as a medium for working
with young people. Activities continue to be the bedrock of youth
work and can be sports- or arts-based, be centred on religion or
politics or concerned with advice and information giving or counselling. Most people bring to their work some particular skill or
interest, be it photography or pot holing, mural painting or moun-
taineering. They need to be enthusiastic about their interest to
capture the attention of others. Such people often become identified
with their own particular brand of work – they are 'arts' people or
'sports' people – and they frequently go to great lengths to improve
or develop skills in their field.

This absorption with one area of work can cast young people in
the role of audience rather than learners. The worker should ensure
that co-workers are selected to counteract this possibility and to
enable young people to have contact with a diverse range of personalities. Otherwise learning will be constrained rather than enhanced
by the youth worker's activities. This is not to denigrate the pursuit
of excellence in specialist areas; but the concern for the personal
development of workers and their training opportunities, while
laudible in its intent, has contributed to this cult of the 'character'.
'Characters' have a particular accomplishment which becomes
honed to such an extent that it becomes all-consuming and takes
centre stage. This changes youth work from being a vehicle for
young people's learning to being a means of meeting the needs of
youth workers.

There is some truth in the notion that people who have had the opportunity to spend time on their own personal development and growth will be more effective workers. However, personal development and training need to be linked more closely to the requirements of the job. More specifically, workers' training should be about how to benefit young people. Otherwise the aura of goodwill, energy and concern to help that is the hallmark of many workers is likely to mask a lack of basic skills in planning and implementing informal education.

The time factor and learning from each other

Informal education in youth work also differs from that of other agencies in that there is often no clear end to a piece of work. The seed of an idea for a project can germinate into a range of activities designed to meet differing needs. Some young people may stay with a project through all the stages in its development. Others will opt in or out at various points. The skills of the worker lie in anticipating some of the outcomes, understanding the nature of the relationship within various peer groups and ensuring that participants have opportunities to reflect upon and learn from their experience. It is in reflecting upon their experience that individuals may learn about their own capacities and apply this knowledge to their own position in society.

The capacity for learning from each other is also a factor that underpins informal education in the Youth Service. Both these characteristics – the time factor and learning from each other – together with the relationship between the personalities of the workers and curriculum construction are illustrated by the following examples drawn from centre-based youth work.

The music workshop

The worker in charge knew there was a great interest in music in the club. One of the senior members was in a band that had just started to get some gigs. The band occasionally rehearsed at the centre and this aroused the interest of members who dropped in to watch. Members of the band felt unsure about letting others loose on their equipment so another way of offering the chance to make music was needed. Eventually a worker, complete with keyboards and acoustic drums, was found. Along with his musical skill came an unconventional appearance, a bit of a 'posh' voice and an evident political awareness. How would members and co-workers react?

It was agreed that it would be insufficient just to provide a music workshop. Time was needed for members to meet the worker and get to know him. For several weeks he came along regularly to the open youth club and sometimes got out the piano and started playing. This aroused a lot of interest. Next came a series of small eye-catching posters around the club advertising a chance for a limited number of members to have a go on keyboard and drums. The first meeting of those interested was set up. The worker declared his terms. The group must include young women and young men and be limited to six. This was duly considered and members countered with some terms of their own. The session sounded too long, they came to the club to do other things as well. A booking system of twenty-minute slots was devised. An atmosphere of negotiation was established. Special interest activities that take place on an open club evening can easily be scuppered by other members or non cooperative staff. In this instance the work done in the preceding weeks reduced the likelihood of this and the music workshop became an accepted part of the club evening.

Conflict soon arose when an unpopular club member booked into the session and was included with members the worker judged most able to handle the situation. Much discussion and argument went on amid the music making but the unpopular member stayed, as did the others. If this were fantasy, the unpopular member would emerge with new friends and understanding. But life is not like that and this did not happen. Nevertheless, all those involved had the chance to reflect on the responsibility they had for their own behaviour and its consequences in relation to other people. The worker, of course, had engineered a lot of what happened. An apparently unstructured event was prepared in a careful and systematic manner. The worker's own skill and interest in music did not override the focus of the session on learning opportunities. A straightforward music workshop, offered as a 'class' rather than as part of the youth club night, would not have made the same input into building relationships before the event. Nor would there have been the same degree of dialogue with the participants. A spin off from this was that the lack of facilities for young people to enjoy hands-on experience of music was brought to the attention of local councillors on the management committee of the centre.

The appeal

The second illustration is related to the time factor which is one of the distinguishing features of informal education in youth work. The youth work curriculum is usually designed as a means of access to learning opportunities rather than as an end in itself. It does not, therefore, slot neatly into the pattern of either timetables or term times.

The appeal certainly did not start out as a carefully structured learning experience. Initially it was a spontaneous individual response to a local fund-raising foundation that resulted in a year long project involving fifty young people. The foundation had a target of £30,000 to be raised for meeting the costs of specialist medical treatment for a local child. The fact that the parents of the child were two ex-club members generated the interest of members and the initial one-off event raised a little money. Once it was clear that this was something that members were keen to support, the youth workers had a close look at the opportunities it could offer for informal education. It was agreed that, in addition to the aim of having fun and raising money, the greater involvement of the members in the club would also be an aim. This was to be monitored and in the course of the year members attended regular meetings, sold tickets, and planned, organized and publicized events. Three members became voluntary helpers in the club, made decisions on the content of events and the ratio of staff to members required.

Throughout the year members tapped in and out of the project and varied the degree of their involvement. The workers encouraged members to learn from each other and there was a high level of interaction among them as skills and experiences were exchanged. For the worker in charge, a local, experienced part-timer with a thorough knowledge of the community, this meant submerging her own fund-raising talents and focusing on the youth work aims of the project. If it had remained a strictly fund-raising affair her organizational skills alone could have raised more money in a shorter time than the combined efforts of all the club members. She knew that the enjoyment, sense of achievement and increased responsibilities undertaken by some members came from focusing on the content and method of working with each other rather than on fund raising as an activity in itself.

The curriculum content of the project and the way it was implemented were heavily influenced by the knowledge and appreciation the worker in charge had of both young people, the local community and its networks of communication. The time span of the project allowed the young people involved to develop their individual commitment at their own pace. For some this involvement was superficial. Others responded to the timely interventions of the workers by becoming involved in action within their community. This heightened their understanding of wider issues, of a National Health Service powerless to support a local family and the awareness that parenting made emotional demands far beyond the ephemeral pleasures of a baby to dress up and show off. More specifically, members displayed an increasing ability to cooperate with others, to make decisions and consider their implications. They demonstrated organizational ability and handled money and publicity responsibly.

Informal education and adolescence

The illustrations above are drawn from the stuff of which centre-based youth work is made, the week-by-week pattern of youth club activities. There is another aspect to the relationship between the personality of the informal educator and the construction and implementation of the curriculum which has more serious implications for the way it affects young people. This is the link between the prevailing views of adolescence and the way young people experience the world. There is a sense in which concepts of adolescence which emphasize its transitory and developmental nature influence a style of youth work geared towards enabling young people to 'get through' it and emerge at the other end as worthy citizens. This sort of youth work has in many ways become indistinguishable from social and life-skills training and is committed to coping with life as it is, accepting it rather than making any critical response.

Life-skills training focuses on individuals and their personal effectiveness. It suggests that individuals are responsible for what happens to them and offers a deficit model of adolescence that needs to be made good by training. It does little to validate young people's own experience and values them for what they might become rather than for what they are. The political issues that shape our lives are ignored. A youth work curriculum that leans this way rejects the life experience of young people and ignores the external factors that limit their horizons.

Theories of adolescence tend to regard teenagers as one homogeneous group. Of course they are not. Adolescents as a group may well be the corporate victims of political and economic strategies that result in a shared experience of unemployment, for example. But even a large-scale issue such as this is experienced differently according to class, race and gender. If a youth work curriculum is to contribute towards the transition from adolescent to adult, then it must turn away from a life-skills training approach and centre on the educational processes involved in increasing political awareness and taking collective action against forms of oppression that constrain young people. Such a curriculum cannot be constructed or implemented by workers unable to relate to young people's experience of the world or connect that experience to the political forces that limit young people's development. Empathy of itself is not sufficient: a worker cannot become a sort of 'honorary' young person by merely understanding the feelings of young people. Political education is the key that can unlock the process of working in an effective way. One of the clearest examples of such a curriculum is to be found in the development of work with girls and young women within the Youth Service. Within this curriculum informal education is characterized by a high level of dialogue between the learners and the educators and an active appreciation of the way young women experience the world (see also Francis in this volume).

The Girls' Club movement was a major casualty of the professionalization of the Youth Service referred to earlier. Early training courses were male strongholds and it is only in recent years that a commitment to a more equitable gender and race balance of students on training courses has emerged. Work with girls and young women does not generally start with the premise of a deficit model of adolescence; it has evolved through the collective experience of the oppression of girls and women in society. The girls' work curriculum is one that centres around common aspects of the lives of the learners and educators and focuses on collective action. The shared experience of fear for safety, for instance, may result in the incorporation of assertiveness training and self-defence instruction in the curriculum. Such action by young women can extend their range of opportunities within the Youth Service and, by challenging the power relationships within that Service, has contributed to a reallocation of resources.

Strengthening the curriculum content?

Can the relationship between the personality of the educator and the curriculum be used to strengthen the curriculum content? There is a danger here that focusing on curriculum content will result in its prescription. If the curriculum in youth work is intended to provide a means of access to informal education, as has been suggested, then particular attention must be paid to the process.

The Youth Service remains one which young people come to voluntarily and which they use on their own terms, which may or may not include thoughts of learning or education. A too clearly defined curriculum is the antithesis of the concept of participation which is enshrined in so much Youth Service thinking. Where attention has been paid to the curriculum in youth work, it has too often been at a remove from practice rather than evolving from it; constructed, for example, as in-service training and slotted into existing provision.

Content can be strengthened by paying attention to the relationship between curriculum and the informal educator. Workers need to be able to draw on and appreciate the world of young people; to have a sense of direction in their work rather than a concern for the minutiae of content. Content will fall into place if there is a dialogue between learners and educators. The multifaceted role of many workers results in poor deployment of human resources. As a consequence they spend a disproportionate amount of time on the administrative tasks associated with the running of a building and liaising between different user groups (Stone 1987). The particular skills workers have in operating with young people can suffer from lack of application, and the cutting edge of political awareness is easily blunted by struggles with bureaucracy. It is not detailed attention to content that is needed but an understanding of the processes of how people learn and a comprehension of the political and social context that shape their lives. A clear sense of purpose facilitates the confidence that allows for continuous critical analysis of the effectiveness of informal education provision within the Youth Service.

Informal education in the Youth Service should remain pioneering and challenging. The performers who cast learners in the role of audience must give way to those workers whose informal education practice is underpinned by a philosophy of political education.

CHAPTER 3

Informal education in residential work with adults

MAL BLACKBURN AND DON BLACKBURN

The two central themes of this chapter, informal education and residential work, are often used as catch alls into which a range of practices and theories are made to fit. Our intention is to offer a partial view, while arguing that there is a coherent relationship between them. This involves briefly examining the development of residential provision and the subsequent debates over community care. In considering residential care the focus will be upon provision for adults categorized as having severe learning difficulties. This term is used rather than 'mental handicap', or the more pejorative 'severely subnormal'. Alternatives occur only in a historical context.

The rise of residential care

The provision of residential care for people with severe learning difficulties began before the asylums and poor law institutions of the nineteenth century. Residential provision was regarded as a model solution to the problem of controlling this group. Segregation of people with severe learning difficulties in institutions enabled the regulation of their relationships with each other and the community. It was sustained by a belief that disability was permanent, young people with such difficulties being removed from school- ing altogether, categorized as ineducable but possibly amenable to training.

Conditions within the institutions were poor. Most were built in the countryside, isolating their occupants from the rest of society. With the development of health and welfare services after 1944, provision of residential care for people with severe learning difficul- ties became the responsibility of the NHS. It inherited the existing problems of overcrowding, underfunding and inadequate education and training for staff. No medical justification for NHS control existed, since severe learning difficulties were not a disease or illness. In a climate of competition for scarce resources within the service, the only form of attention given this client group was all too often the management of basic physical needs. A series of reports in the 1960s and 1970s subsequently revealed the extent of the squalor in which many were living. Such reports catalogued a disturbing number of acts of callousness and brutality by staff (HMSO 1969, 1971a; Morris 1969).

The consequences of the custodial system can be seen in a number of ways. The assumptions which accompany it are that the task is relatively simple, requiring minor consideration, and that the accompanying skills needed, demand little development. Jones (1975) discovered these views among qualified as well as unqualified staff in a large hospital for people with severe learning difficulties. Of the qualified staff 65 per cent, and 93 per cent of the unqualified, agreed that 'When looking after patients, ability and common-sense are more important than formal training' (*ibid*: 87). In addition, 74 per cent of all staff agreed that 'Kindness is more important than a therapeutic programme for patients' (*ibid*: 88).

The task of the worker in this environment can be seen to have three components: to attend to the bodily needs of the resident; to ensure that the procedures of the institution are followed and rules are obeyed; and to accomplish this in a way which, as far as possible, does not make the residents unhappy. The worker is overwhelmingly engaged in managing the conformity of the residents, in the application of a control system appropriate to a factory or barracks, except that in this case there is no compensating pay for those living under the discipline of the regime. Training clearly has a purpose in this framework and as Goffman has remarked 'we forget how detailed and restrictive it can become in total institutions' (1961: 43).

The critique of this system must avoid merely blaming the caretakers for the dehumanizing and inhumane practices which developed in much residential work. This is not to defend brutality or callousness on anyone's part. However, the staff themselves were enmeshed in the same ideology as the residents, both in their work and in the way their education was perceived. The structure of the NHS is hierarchical, with the lower tiers not only expected, but required, to defer to those above. Hierarchy is marked clearly by power differentials linked to credentials: medical staff are above nursing staff, qualified nurses above the unqualified and patients at the base.

If the tasks of residential care are perceived simply as custodianship plus a modicum of training for residents, then the form of education staff receive will reflect this. The acquisition of skills in the processes of bodily care will be emphasized, alongside a knowledge of the rules of the institution. Workers cannot be involved in reflection upon the justification of rules and procedures (i.e. the 'content' of training for residents) since that would undermine the authority relationships on which the organizational edifice depends. If we regard the development of critical reflection as a central component of the educational process, then the programme has to be seen as training as opposed to education.

It might be argued that even within such a framework reflection is possible. For example, workers could be encouraged to consider changes to training programmes where the efficiency of the institution might be raised. Improvements in training people with severe learning difficulties to take care of their own bodily needs might be justified on grounds of efficiency and cost-effectiveness. However, the restrictions upon workers' criticism of the techniques of training merely reinforce the control emphasis of the system. What ought to be reflected upon is the purpose, content and social relationships of the programme. Otherwise it remains related to the needs of the institution and not to those of the workers or residents involved.

A training emphasis rather than an educational approach means that the methods applied to the residents can be applied in the same form to everyone. Because the subject matter is the same for all, i.e. the rule system, or daily living routines, it can be assumed that they may be learnt in an identical way. If the training programme can be applied uniformly, then the trainers can be taught the method uniformly. It is not merely the content of training programmes that is placed beyond critique by the workers: the form of their own training and their own practice is also set beyond their reach. So a division is created between theory and practice. The organizational structure discourages reflection, while the workers' own training is not conducive to the development of theory. Given this alienating system, staff find it difficult to respond to the residents' educational needs, that is their cognitive, emotional, social and physical development.

The shift to community care

Donges (1982) concluded that residential care based on central government direction had, for this group of people, failed. The alternative of locally organized services was preferable even though there might be a cost in terms of a lack of coordination between different initiatives. The range of provision described as 'residential care' was becoming more flexible, stretching from ordinary houses in the community to larger purpose-built units, as well as more traditional forms of accommodation. Underpinning the movement to community care was a more optimistic view of the possibilities for education and training. Rather than seeing severe learning difficulties as a static condition, the environment or context within which the person lived was now assumed to have a significant impact on individual development. The 1971 White Paper (HMSO 1971b) reflected this when it argued for a planned response to the assessed needs of individuals, with the involvement of families in the assessment process.

The Barclay Report went further (NISW 1980: 62):

> clients' preferences and perceptions of their own needs should always be taken seriously when admission to either residential or day care is being considered; there should be a continuing dialogue between clients and service providers about needs and preferences.

The concept of development involved here was more concerned with education than with training. It recognized that change is possible in the individual. The goals of the programme were implicitly flexible, with both individuals and their families being involved in their specification. This implied that the methods of teaching would be sufficiently flexible to reflect the range of goals identified.

The Barclay Report recommended that residential care should not only provide basic physical well-being but also group and individual experiences which were satisfying and contributed to learning and development. The commitment to continuity of care, through the maintenance of links with other service networks, could be facilitated with a key worker system, the key worker being a named member of staff with responsibility for ensuring that the resident's needs as a whole were met. This was considered to be particularly important when several agencies might be involved in delivery.

A rather non-problematic view of care in the community has often been propagated. According to this view an individual is able, as a result of a carefully constructed programme of training, to make the transition from institution to the kind of everyday life that other people are assumed to enjoy (Gunzberg 1963; Kiernan and Jones 1977; Jeffree and Cheseldine 1982; Whelan 1984). But the individual programme designed to teach the skills and knowledge which it is assumed are required can have more to do with the expectations of others than with the expressed wishes of the individual. The formal training programme becomes an obstacle course for the individual to traverse before release. When the programme is completed the transition can be made. The individual is expected to change to meet the criterion of 'normality', rather than the community being expected to demonstrate tolerance.

Behaviourist approaches

The methodology which has gained widespread favour in the construction of programmes for people with severe learning difficulty is based to a considerable extent on behaviourism. According to Woods and Shears (1986), the latter has become orthodoxy in relation to the education and training of young people and adults with severe learning difficulties. It offers a particular conceptualization of the goals and methodology of the teaching programme. Goals are specified in terms of the observable behaviours which a student will carry out at the end of the programme. Method is related to the reinforcement of the desired behaviours. This process is legitimated by the claim that people with severe learning difficulties do not learn spontaneously from experience (Mittler 1979; Fenn 1976; Gardner *et al.* 1983). Systematic teaching is therefore required. There are a number of objections to this, not least the validity of the evidence on which the statement is based. It also often contains the rider 'unlike normal children', thus implying a significant difference in the learning patterns of people with severe learning difficulties. Even if the statement were true, it would not necessarily follow that 'systematic teaching' is equivalent to behavioural approaches: indeed, it is difficult to conceive of teaching which is not systematic. If an activity does not have some purpose and procedure it can hardly be described as teaching.

Alongside the rhetoric has developed a plethora of 'curricula', which consist of lists of behaviours which are assumed to comprise the skills required for independent living. A central difficulty here is the conflict between the stated aims of such programmes, those of autonomy and independence, and the technological rationality which underpins the managerial programme. Woods and Shears (1986) have pointed to the facile conception of independence which behaviourists put forward. The autonomy of the person is perceived as an accumulation of skills and behaviours – a Legoland model of human development. It appears to be little more than a barely sophisticated version of the habit-training programmes of the large institutions. These programmes contribute to a process of deskilling the educators. Little thought or reflection need be given to goals since the lists of behaviours are preset.

Such technology is legitimated by its effectiveness. The behaviour described on the checklist is observed in the trainee at the end of the programme and the programme thus appears to justify itself. The efficiency rating accrued invariably appeals to managements everywhere; the effectiveness of staff becomes amenable to evaluation; and the cost of genuine staff education and development avoided. The niggling snags that remain are explained away by the nature of the learning difficulties of the trainee. Shortcomings in the transference of the skills acquired to novel contexts are portrayed not as the fault of the approach but as a consequence of severe learning difficulty.

Normalization programmes and the use of the informal

An alternative to the above practice has been described by Bank-Mikkelsen (1976) as 'normalization'. If learning is to take place, the service should provide a minimally restrictive environment rather than 'normalizing' the resident. Within this model, people with severe learning difficulties live in small units within the community. Support is provided by staff to enable the occupants to develop their full potential and take an active part in the neighbourhood in which they live. This approach genuinely involves individuals in setting their own goals for learning. When carried out in ordinary daily living situations they have the opportunity to reflect upon their own performance and the basis for grounded intervention becomes clear. In this sense the educational process is informal.

Although the goals of the programme can broadly be defined in advance, the chance to acquire the knowledge, abilities and attitudes needed for living in the community will depend on the wishes of the person and the opportunities which present themselves. For example, there are clearly a finite number of ways of greeting other people; but the appropriateness of action can be judged only in a real context. The learning of a repertoire of actions to greet other people should be developed through reflection on experience.

The term 'informal education' in the context of residential work is used to indicate the negotiability of the process, both content and method. But this does not necessarily mean that residents should be left to their own devices when the programme is under way. Unfortunately, the concept of informal education has too frequently been invoked to utilize an individualistic perception of the learning process, where the student is expected to interact with the context and create understanding without help.

Informal education and residential work

As far as informal education in residential work is concerned, the negotiable aspects of the programme are genuinely that. This does *not* mean that the residential workers abrogates responsibility to be involved in that negotiation. In reality the worker is involved in, and is part of, the context in which the resident lives and about which he or she is learning. The extent to which it is possible for residents to have control over, and learn about, their own abilities, will be constrained in part by the way that the workers choose to act or are allowed to act by the organizational structure.

If freedom of choice is not available in what the resident does, then this is clearly a recipe for institutionalization. This can be simply illustrated by considering the everyday activities of people within residential agencies. The resident may be faced with a routine at breakfast time which has the tables set (perhaps the previous evening), the choice of food limited to staff-selected cereals on the table and even the seating arrangements ordered by the workers. The space for the resident to display initiative and choice is curtailed. There is no need or opportunity for the resident to select the crockery or be involved in food preparation.

Issues like this are often regarded as trivial and hardly worth consideration in a discussion of responses to need. However, it is in these very areas that the institutionalization of people is at its most powerful. How can individuals learn to act in appropriate ways when they have little experience of taking control over the fairly mundane aspects of their own existence? The routines of residential settings can in many cases prove to be the most difficult to change; yet the content of the learning programme is often concerned with precisely such daily activities.

Routines often operate as a consequence of the organization's needs and limited staffing cover. There is pressure to standardize responses to need in the interests of efficiency. This can affect all aspects of daily lives from the timetable of activities to the menu. The involvement of residents in making choices and decisions clearly conflicts with standardized care. There may also be pressure on staff to ensure that the range of tasks involved in caring for people who may have a high dependency are completed during their time on duty. In the short term, involving residents in learning to do things for themselves can be more time consuming than the staff performing those tasks themselves. This particular issue is highlighted by Shearer in her discussion of the relationship between professionals and disabled people and is one that she describes as being based on a 'cycle of expectation': '. . . residential staff can be handicapped by their assumption that people whose disabilities are as severe as this "ought" to be a candidate for their care' (1981: 109). This tendency to make the client dependent on the staff and establishment was also addressed in a study by Rosen (1972) who found that many self-care tasks were performed by staff rather than allowing people with severe learning difficulties to learn for themselves. The assumptions and beliefs about severe learning difficulties can clearly be as constraining within voluntary and local authority provision as they ever were within the health service framework. In this sense, then, an informal educational approach necessitates a move away from an organizationally defined routine to one based upon individual needs, which can then provide everyday activities as opportunities for learning to make judgements and choices.

The routines of residential work have also traditionally influenced the way that staff job descriptions have been constructed. Staff have been largely seen as unskilled or semi-skilled manual workers, with a demarcation between carers, cleaners, cooks and officers. Staff-training needs within this framework have been seen as relating to the task-based job descriptions. However, a system which was based upon an educational approach to residential work would necessitate the removal of these task-based distinctions between staff, since all should be concerned with the skilled work of facilitating the development of residents rather than the routine tasks of the institution.

In addition to the organizational constraints on staff, and assumptions about disability, the taken-for-granted nature of everyday activities can place them beyond question. It can be challenging enough for staff to develop alternatives to well-established practices and routines if they themselves have little power and the routines are strongly legitimated by apparently better qualified and experienced staff. It is difficult to be critical in a clean, well-ordered setting with friendly relationships and good quality food. Staff may themselves have beliefs and values about the way in which everyday events should be ordered and how individuals should act. These may range from the times at which events should take place to the way residents should eat. A critical approach to the values and practices of the agency cannot be divorced from a similar approach to one's own values and practice. This is intrinsic to the informal education of staff.

The concept of care is inadequate if it remains at the level of providing good hotel facilities as a response to the needs of individuals. Care has to be based on a dynamic understanding which accommodates the development of individuals as social beings, able to learn to take control over their own affairs. This has implications for residential settings in that the opportunity to manage many, if not all, of the aspects of the setting should be afforded to residents and not merely restricted to some of those defined as staff. If staff themselves have little control within the establishment how can they be expected to involve residents in this process? An informal educational approach, with its implied notion of developing autonomy for residents, requires flexible management structures, with in-built opportunities for decision making by all staff and residents.

There is thus a clear relationship between the educational needs of staff and those of residents, a point underlined by the Wagner Report (HMSO 1988a: 89).

> We see the goals of an effective staff development and training policy as being . . . an ethos in which the needs and interests of the residents are paramount. This in turn requires the staff to be constantly seeking to change and adapt their own responses to the changing and varied needs of the residents. It further requires a commitment by staff members to learning as a continuous process . . .

The development of residents and staff are not simply related, in this argument, but are in fact dependent on each other. The recommendations of the Wagner Report (*ibid*: 67–8) emphasize this mutual relationship. The review of research for the report (Atkinson 1988) also reinforces the need for delegation of responsibility to, and autonomy of, care staff in providing a high quality service. This is to be set within the context of clear policies and a statement of aims and values for the agency.

The necessity for an informal approach is related to the self-confidence and self-image of the resident. The relationship of the worker to the resident is not envisaged here to be merely that of instructor. It is not sufficient for residents to demonstrate competence at particular tasks to satisfy the appraisal of a staff member. An approach to education based upon a training model involves an implicit power relationship between the trainer and trainee. The competence of the former is contrasted with the incompetence of the latter. The differential between the two is not merely one of skills but is also related to self-confidence. Brown has shown in one study that people with learning difficulties 'could not resist even mild social pressure, even though they showed competence in many vocational and social skill areas' (1977: 392). A subsequent programme involving informal decision making markedly improved the performance of people in this respect.

This issue has not necessarily been addressed by recent developments. Much of the contemporary debate has injected a welcome focus on the needs of individuals and their involvement in the planning of agency responses. The construction of Individual Programme Plans (IPP) has been seen by some agencies as one way of organizing this process. However, the IPP approach has also often included an assessment framework, based upon the kind of behavioural schedules outlined above. Although people with learning difficulties may be involved in a choice of educational goals when constructing an IPP, the choice is effectively constrained by the menu of skills provided in the assessment. Where these assessments have been adopted for use across a local authority, there would seem to be a rather ironic relationship between the conception of individuality set within a standardized review of need. Implied by this process is not merely a lack of competence in living skills but also an inability on the part of people with learning difficulties to make judgements about their own needs. In addition, the conception of individuality is not set within a social framework. Autonomy is concerned not merely with behaving as other people expect but with choosing to act in ways which are consonant with one's own knowledge, understanding and beliefs about both self and society. Education and development are fundamentally social in terms of the knowledge involved and the opportunities which are available to choose to act.

The move to community care and the emphasis on education is, therefore, not necessarily marked by increased independence and autonomy for the person with severe learning difficulties. In fact it highlights the tensions within the residential task between the need to educate and the need to protect. The strategy of community care necessarily brings this conflict into the open. Education for independence involves an element of risk taking which can only be assessed in practice and for which there can be few standardized procedures. The first time an individual crosses the road without supervision or uses public transport, the outcome cannot be specified with certainty. Staff themselves need the confidence to engage in this kind of risk taking.

The low status of the residential contribution

The fact that it has been difficult for residential staff to develop either their own skills and knowledge, or the quality of service in this field may be due in part to the low esteem the work has amongst other professionals. As Barclay stated (NISW 1980: 52),

> many social workers in the field regard it as one of their primary objectives to keep people out of residential establishments wherever possible. Yet a person who leaves home for another place remains the same person, with the same human needs and the same emotional links with the family or community.

The negative view of residential provision within social work is explored by Davis (1981). The author argues that this perception of residential work is reflected not only in the low status of staff and residents but also in the lack of training opportunities for staff. In fact more than 80 per cent of staff in residential work had no relevant qualification at the time of the Barclay Report (1980). This situation has not significantly altered in the intervening period.

> Of residential and day care staff, only 7.5 per cent working with adults and 11.5 per cent working with children have a social work qualification; these percentages increase to 24 per cent and 34 per cent respectively if non-social work qualification, e.g. in teaching or nursing are included. These figures compare with 57 per cent in field social work who have a social work qualification, and 71.5 per cent when other qualifications are included.

HMSO 1988a: 87

It may be argued that this is a consequence of residential provision in a segregated environment still being seen as an end in itself. In other words, the role of staff remains wholly or mainly custodial. Another factor may be the necessity for sponsorship by local social services in order for staff to have access to many of the educational programmes in social work. There is little possibility of staff engaging in educational programmes on their own initiative. Governmental constraints on local authority spending may also have resulted in authorities placing different priorities on the education of workers in the various social work sectors.

The Wagner Report also commented upon the links between the low esteem in which residential work is held and the educational needs of workers in this area.

It would seem that many courses for the Certificate of Qualification in Social Work (CQSW) have yet to develop programmes that meet the specific learning needs of prospective residential practitioners.

HMSO 1988a: 85

The Report argues that the factors involved in determining the status of residential work are material ones in the first instance (Chapter 8.13, Chapter 9.2). It goes on to point to the double bind that this can create in responding to the educational needs of the staff (85): 'Regrettably, because of the failure to improve the standing of residential work, a CQSW is seen as a passport out from low status and low paid work, involving unsocial hours'.

Given this lack of opportunity, it is difficult to see how staff can construct a critical practice or develop their own work. The perception of the job as an end, rather than a means towards development, combined with the managerial approach to training both residents and staff, reinforces the powerlessness of both groups to affect change. The informal education of staff at work in developing a reflective and dynamic practice has to be reinforced by an extension of the more formal educational opportunities leading to credentials through an extension of access to further and higher education. It is also necessary for staff in institutions of further and higher education to take seriously the possibility that informal education of staff in residential work might be recognized as a valid route to some form of credential.

This chapter has examined the relationship between education and residential care for people with severe learning difficulty. It has argued that changes in that provision and practice reflect shifting definitions of need, which in their turn may reflect differing ideologies about the nature of human development. In this process the educational needs of both staff and residents can be seen to be interdependent and should be underpinned by the same principles. An educational approach, whether formal or informal, is essentially optimistic about the possibility of people developing understanding and control over both their own activities and their social context.

Until the 1960s practice was legitimated by the belief that people with severe learning difficulties were unlikely to develop in response to either education or a nurturing environment. Recent practice is now linked to the assumption that development is possible, given the right conditions and opportunities. However, the particular form of much of what is described as 'education' for people with severe learning difficulties bears a strong resemblance to the older training perspective which accompanied institutional provision. The way that the needs of people are defined has changed radically and is still evolving. Whether the right conditions and opportunities can be offered in relation to both education and residential provision is a question which needs to be addressed both at the level of the individual worker and at that of policy making. It is a moot point in this process whether the use of the term education, informal or otherwise, has received sufficient critical attention in recent developments.

CHAPTER 4

Informal education with young women in the community

GLYNIS FRANCIS

This chapter will focus on my work as an educator within the community rather than as a trainer in a formal educational institution. For it is through my work within the community that I have primarily developed my philosophical and political thinking on education and not the other way around. My basic premise is that all people value educational opportunities. We all know what it feels like to experience the power of knowledge either as a positive, because we have it, or as a negative because we do not.

Educational opportunities are most commonly seen as being time at school and perhaps college; a time that is culturally largely predetermined and economically shaped. The curriculum for these educational opportunities is generally speaking outside of the control of the participants. Much research and debate has focused on how children learn, or learn to fail. In many respects, the problems arise from a desire to socialize people, to prepare pupils and students to be acquiescent citizens with knowledge and vision, not thinking individuals. The authoritarianism of much formal education contrasts with the belief of many community workers that 'we are here to respond to the needs of the people'. This view has been less frequently encountered since the decline of the people-centred politics of the 1960s and 1970s. Community action in this country had its heyday during those decades, spurred on by political activists from within communities and student bodies without. Tenants' associations and campaigns for better housing, fairer rents, play facilities, work conditions and community resources later became integrated and institutionalized. However, where there was money and resources, there was also accountability and strings.

The growth of community development teams during this period shifted the focus from action to reform. The intervention of professionals, people employed and paid directly or indirectly by the state, challenged the power base within communities. The lack of clarity within which this intervention often took place served to fog the debates. People's perceived needs were reinterpreted by professionals and the practical outcome, stereotypically, were the community associations, mums-and-toddlers' groups and play schemes now to be found in most inner city areas. In this context training is often provided to ensure that community members perform their tasks more skilfully and develop an awareness of the differences within a community and respect for individuals. The real challenges, as I have seen them, are not in creating the appropriate learning environment or marketing courses: rather, they relate to selling a philosophical and political perspective that challenges the notions of the educated and the status of learning materials; undermines the assumed professional status of teachers; and strives to put the learners in control of their learning.

The experience of being an informal educator

It is difficult to communicate the freshness and excitement I have felt about education. I feel restrained by the language used to rationalize and give meaning to educational experiences by educationalists – estranged from the process and definitions generally available because of a differing value base. For some time the basis of my work seemed like a reaction to the structures and attitudes found within formal education, the sense of relative powerlessness, the consumption of the prescribed cake with humbleness and gratitude. With a respect for my own struggle through the system I had to move and define some principles for myself as an informal educator.

When appointed as a neighbourhood worker attached to a large community school and college, I was very impressed with the resources available. What I had not appreciated was the struggle there would be to utilize them, both in terms of gaining access for community groups and in releasing them to be taken out into the community. I was probably appointed to the job, in part, for my warmth, openness, energy and enthusiasm: a sort of human minibus, with a big purse, a coal fire and comfy chair and the stamp of approval saying 'where there's a will there's a way'. The key resource, and sometimes the only resource, for work within the community are workers themselves. Learning how to manage myself, as a valuable resource, became the hardest task. To make sense of these ideas I will describe a number of situations which have caused me to examine my practice and adjust my thinking.

A key learning stage for me was associated with the development of a project for truants, who preferred the atmosphere of the adventure playground to the local community school. In the view of the New Romantics people should be free to learn when and where they want. In sympathy with such an approach I spent a considerable amount of time trying to make contact with these young people. The first hurdle was to get them to stand still long enough to let them know I was not a teacher, wag officer, social worker or plain-clothed police-woman. So much for my alternative image.

The next hurdle was to give them some reason for a working contact. Here the choice of roles is enormous. If you are too entertaining then what do you really know? Too authoritarian, then you are just like the rest. Interesting, respectful and fair, then you are unreal and short-lived. The third hurdle is the potential for role conflict with other young people and colleagues. The style of relationship offered to young people was a step towards empowerment. It involved establishing roles and interests without the power, traditions and status which can be called upon by those working in mainstream educational settings. In practice, this involved using a range of detached youth work skills which are not properly understood or shared by other professions. Contact made with young people on their own territory, to some extent on their terms, enabled me to have a quite different perception of their needs, a greater awareness of the circumstances surrounding their lives, and indeed some empathy with truanting. An additional difficulty was that the working contract with these young people legitimized their time with the project outside school, yet in school hours.

Every social and liberation movement threatens some other group's values, assumptions and power, which inevitably leads to a questioning of the nature, struggle and distribution of power and authority in society. The main objection from the teaching staff was that the project's influence might encourage truanting, that the level of empathy shown to young people could undermine the attempts of teachers to deal with it. And, indeed, young people might gain some power from their new perceptions and understandings, thus undermining the teaching staff in what they saw as the right and best way to educate young people.

Another crucial question was who controls and sets the curriculum or the agenda for learning. I had been working with small groups of young women and girls in the neighbourhood centre. The objective was to develop a lunch-time session catering particularly for students and those without work. The session took the form of a discussion group in the club, sometimes sparked off by a video or speaker. The agenda, as I saw it, was to encourage discussion about women's issues such as abortion, rape, marriage and sexuality. I consciously directed the choice of subjects for discussion to embrace women's perspectives and feminist ideas. These sessions were very popular, despite the interference of the lads. However, the main challenges came from other youth and community staff who questioned the choice of topics and accused me, and others, of trying to brainwash young women and impose ideas on them. The issue here was that I saw myself as having an educator's role which involved the presentation of a female and feminist perspective on topics, not my personal perspective. Although the two are clearly linked, extending understanding of different values, challenging ideas and thoughts, are crucial activities for educators seeking to get people thinking and questioning. It is important to acknowledge and recognize the subjective elements and ensure a counterbalance. This can be achieved by providing information, access to knowledge and understanding, in order to create the possibility of choice for others. The question here is whether we will become unpopular if we state or propose the agenda or curriculum. Are we simply 'entertainers' rather than the 'lion tamers' (schoolteachers), who perceive ourselves as better people because we care about individuals?

Within the formal structure my role as a neighbourhood worker had an air of casualness: I was not restricted by bells and timetables. I was on first-name terms with young people and had a responsibility to be out in the community. The fact that I worked evenings, weekends and school holidays was hidden from the teaching staff. Having a choice of roles is like having a wardrobe of clothes. It is nice to know you have a choice, but how easy is it to make it? Within the centre I could take advantage of the role young people – students and pupils – were expected to play and the 'normal' behaviour expected of them. I was able to command similar authority to the teaching staff in school. The risk was that young people would then be unable to see me in a different role outside school. Out on the streets and around the neighbourhood I was able to change my behaviour without immediately exposing the role boundaries of the centre staff. Given the 'exposed' nature of neighbourhood work, having to rely on your own abilities without the security of the institution and its labels, the risk of losing confidence and clarity of purpose is high. One personal strategy was to align myself with other people in similar roles encountering similar risks, like adventure playground workers, community leaders and the national detached youth workers' forum.

Informal education and social relations

> Bored, lonely, looking for a challenge why not call into your local Community Education Centre and see what we have to offer . . . short courses for all members of the community . . . pay as you learn . . . from Play and your Under 5s to pre-retirement courses . . . from local history to aerobics.

All these activities have a potential educational value for the participants. Recruitment processes are crucial in ensuring that the opportunity reflects the needs and interests of the people. The community education centre, in offering opportunities 'from cradle to grave', seeks to connect with fundamental aspects of life, to develop education from the processes of production of our lives. And in these processes of production, women occupy a particular and often hidden and subordinated role. Community education touches on these social relations and derives some of its power from them. Educational practice may reinforce existing social relations or it may undermine them. It does not escape them.

How is it that uniformed organizations have the membership that they do and that church and local groups continue to attract people? These institutions have a long history, based largely on voluntary effort, are deep-rooted in tradition and overtly concerned with moral and social well-being. In my analysis belief in sisterhood, brotherhood, the family and an acceptance of role, indicates that the need for belonging, importance, worth and respect continues to be a basic need. As someone brought up in a village. I took my place within the church, belonged to the Girl Guides, was the eldest child in my family and attended the nearest secondary modern school for girls – or young ladies, as our head teacher reminded us weekly. These were all age-old institutions with women at the helm.

Twenty years on personal and social education is dominated by women; most community education tutors I know are women, and within youth clubs and organizations women so often seem to hold the key roles. The reason for drawing the reader's attention to this is to suggest that within the broadest definition of informal education, social relations are one of the most important areas for consideration. Women have been socialized into caring roles and they are a majority in the caring professions. This underpins women's social interaction both professionally and personally. Women can find themselves devalued because their tasks and skills are not seen as scientific or intellectual. So while women remain the guardians of human rights, men control the means of production.

Government policies continue to legislate traditional roles and values for men and women and to emphasize the centrality of the family. Yet although the national trend has pulled in one direction it has still been exciting to see, and be a part of, a decade of developments which have sought to extend opportunities for girls and young women. Equal opportunity policies have been useful – insofar as the paper on which they are written can offer some protection. Management and officers are able to state their intentions and fend off unwanted criticism. However, women's skills and abilities can be professionalized at one point and be made redundant, except as a cottage industry, the next. Equal opportunity policies have followed the traditional pattern of decision making. They have been delivered and administered from the top down, reaffirming the traditional and existing social order and relations.

Young women and informal education

Here I want to begin by focusing on some of the work I have undertaken with young mothers. Young women who choose to become mothers do so for a number of reasons. Motherhood can be a role that bridges the divide between schoolgirl and adult worker. The first of these is compulsory, the second may be unobtainable, at least if young women want to retain some element of self-respect and integrity. Motherhood has a clear role and status, leading to unpaid work, that at least allows for some self-expression such as a beautifully cared for baby. Baby putting on weight can be experienced as a personal achievement; taking her first step, uttering her first words. The happy, playful and developing child meets with the approval of health visitor, clinic and family, all of whom reinforce the achievement of 'successful motherhood'. This means that women can make the role of mother their primary concern for many years; other can feel themselves to have the potential which only needs discovering. Young women, particularly those with small children are being judged, assessed, observed and recorded as a sociological phenomenon. The media has done much to damage the self-esteem and confidence of young mothers. Headlines such as 'Gymslip mums', 'Teenage pregnancies' seek to provoke disquiet and feed further moral panic.

My approach to these young women was based on an assumption that they were not making use of the local mums-and-toddlers' groups, mainly for fear of being judged as inadequate or viewed as irresponsible for having a child outside marriage. My contact with these young women was initially on the streets and through the health clinic. It was my intention to offer a variety of skills and experience that would be useful in terms of their independence and in relation to their roles as mothers.

After our first few meetings the young women were able to identify some learning needs of their own, such as the role of child guidance, how to choose a primary school, child development and how parents can help, basic do-it-yourself skills, sport and outdoor pursuits and how to secure and organize a holiday away. Using their position as mothers we were able to look more widely at the role of women in society and the different pressures upon us. The Young women had a variety of experiences and attitudes to raising children and the role of mothers. They were particularly fearsome of social workers and health visitors and wanted to know more about their legal position and the functions these professionals performed.

The content of sessions was negotiated with the young women and as group worker I encouraged them to question and challenge what was being said. All the while I drew on my own experience as a single-parent, lesbian mother to provide a challenge to the notion of the nuclear family being the only right environment in which to raise children. One particular attitude that prevailed was that having had a child it was your responsibility to provide for it. In practice, these young women were initially very reluctant to leave their children in the creche or seek a place in a nursery. It was a real achievement when, after running a series of rock-climbing sessions, discussion groups, learning to use video camera with the children 'in tow', some young women decided to leave their children in the creche. Only then could they begin to express their spirit and optimism as young women with wants and needs of their own. The project did not succeed in maintaining the interest and involvement of all the young women. Those that left were critical of the behaviour of others in relation to their children. Some did not want to be identified with single mothers and felt themselves to be better off and hence not in need of the support or activities on offer.

Young women had been attracted to the various groups and provision because of the possibility of getting what they wanted in the way of advice, association, activities, action and access. The facilities were made available for their exclusive or primary use on

Glynis Francis

the basis that separate provision should be a choice within communities. As far as was possible and practicable, child care was provided
and the space made warm, comfortable and welcoming. So certain
boundaries were established by workers and the agency, both
philosophically and physically. The next stage related to the assessment by the young women, of skills, knowledge and resources
which should be given priority. It is this political step that tests most
fundamentally those educators who believe in the expansion of
educational opportunities. Much of this style of intervention is
summed up in the words 'relevant and meaningful', which must be
central to our agenda as informal educators. To be relevant and
meaningful is to negotiate, reflect needs, individualize, personalize.
Yet to have meaning this must be linked to participation, democracy
and community development.

In the past participant democracies have been seen to rest upon and
even presuppose the existence of small and local groups like family
networks, the neighbourhood, the parish and work groups. Today,
primary groups of this kind are often experienced as less 'close' or
else seem increasingly functionless in an age of centralization and
mobility. Informal education provides the workers with a
framework that ideally attempts, in principle, to engage with people
as equals. I do not mean to suggest that my life as a professional
worker is somehow comparable to that of an unemployed single
parent; but my lack of statutory power and the fact that the young
women chose involvement helped foster an air of equality. The
infrastructure, the family and church, may not exist for these young
women and alternative supportive networks need to be fostered. I
think it is imperative that we do not see ourselves as entertainers, lion
tamers or plain-clothed police or, for that matter, do-gooders with
our basket of goodies. For to do so subscribes to a view that the
people we are educating are deficient or worse, that a good laugh, a
friendly smile or straight talking is somehow going to relieve their
problems.

Prioritizing

Prioritizing by using some hidden criterion is manipulative. Prioritizing by first come, first served ignores inequality of opportunities.
Prioritizing by pretending to a neutral stance is naïve. Prioritizing by
'this is what we have always done, it's worked out all right to now',
maintains the status quo. All prioritizing reflects the political ideologies of those empowered to take action and make such decisions.

For educators working in informal settings, this process entails an awareness of inequalities. Both the worker and agency need to identify areas of need openly and unashamedly. An examination of existing resources and provision, their relevance and appropriateness to the potential user's needs is essential. An appraisal of staff skills and values to create the optimum effectiveness and efficiency of a learning situation is also required. Some groups' needs are easier met than others; for example, disabled people's access to some centres is poor and in reality creates an unsuitable learning environment. The need for prioritization cannot be ignored since the reality of funding for such work is usually aimed at particular areas in the country and related to already identified sections of the community. Limited resources, funding with in-built priorities, political biases and workers' time are all elements that need to be managed, monitored, maintained and developed in response to the priorities identified.

Critical analysis of the educational direction of some developments shows that greater resources, particularly in terms of person power, have been gained for women's and girls' issues in education. A tolerance for separate provision is growing, with some back-up resources. The needs of women now reach the agendas of departments, committees and organizations even if the outcome is undesirable. In some areas women have a higher profile within their community: they are seen as organizers, administrators, campaigners, spokespersons, enablers, winners and fighters. Women's history has been a popular topic within community education; it serves to give a political as well as historical context to women's struggle. Events like International Women's Day have provided a significant focus for some women and have prompted our conscience about the need for international struggle. On the other hand, the higher profile given to some women has alienated some from the working class. A high degree of sensitivity is required when allocating budgets. Positive action not only necessitates clarity of aim and objective but also the building of the support and political power to carry it forward.

The tradition of autonomy and choice within informal education enshrines a philosophy of live and let live. Yet Brownies are seen as respectable, whereas girls' nights are seen as subversive. Young women's projects and the like can initiate a questioning of the nature, structure and distribution of power and authority within the community and society. As a result of differentiation on the basis of age, sex and social status, women are able to debate class, values, attitudes, the lifestyles of different groups, subcultures and counter-cultures and the extent to which differences should be tolerated and accepted. Informal educational opportunities offered to particular groups are important as a counterbalance to the inequalities created and legitimated in most institutions.

Disaffected young women see themselves as failures; their confidence as people is often limited to a few situations. Their ability to understand their position is restricted, the range of social skills on which they draw is narrow, the language they have to communicate with is insufficient and their ability to identify their needs is constrained. So a fundamental stage in opening up educational opportunities to women, and in particular young women, is to help them break through all barriers and blocks to learning, irrespective of whether these relate to feelings, thoughts or ideas.

Placing young women's experiences at the centre

Any methodology that seeks to relate to these young women must put their own experience at the core. 'Girls only' sessions in centres and in the community have been a focus for my work and have provided an opportunity for girls to familiarize themselves with equipment and skills usually dominated by boys. Within these environments girls and young women have explored their relationships with each other as well as their prejudices on class, race, age and sexual identity. Through drama and role play, girls and young women have explored their feelings of anger, violence and frustration. Some have developed strong leadership skills and now contribute in many different ways to activities and the running of the centres.

For the educator the process has been clearly guided by values and principles. It is a conscious and purposeful intervention into the lives of others. We talk cynically about offering carrots to entice our client group, attractive activities used as a vehicle for the 'real' work. It is actually my intention to make the 'content' significant. Advertising a programme of activities for young women to include water skiing, wind surfing, rock climbing, can look attractive. It is unfortunately the case that many young women show interest but feel unable to take the risks involved. A simple statement that says 'rock climbing for young women run by women, equipment provided, creche available, no previous experience required', can go some way towards allaying fears. Our fears, I suspect, are to do with being accused of not working in the interest of the majority; of pursuing our own interests through our work; of raising hopes and expectations in young women that cannot be met and followed through. However, by placing young women and their views at the centre of the process, by engaging in a dialogue with them, such concerns can be contained and practice grounded. So, for example, a hair-dressing session requested by young women came to explore hair care, self-images, the question of who women look good for, diet for health, hair braiding and beading, why some women wanted to straighten their hair, and photography. We also discussed the difference between the Saturday job girl and the professionalizing of hair dressing and beauty therapy. When approaching different areas, I try to widen and deepen understanding.

In working with young women with children there is a wealth of experience to be shared and learnt. By relating fundamental hopes and values to each other, to the lives and experiences of mothers and women before us, not just within Europe but in other parts of the world, we can build a confidence in our abilities and through understanding our position in history gain some sense of freedom to move on. It is a style and approach that encroaches upon conversation and story telling, where by discussing our experiences of school and family we can 'evoke and evaluate our collective memory of what is done to us and what we do in turn' (Russell 1983: 52). Russell goes on to say that story telling is an age-old method of transferring knowledge, skills and values. It gives political value to daily life. No activity is too trivial for political analysis.

The educational pay off for this particular area of community development can be measured in the more traditional ways: take up on college courses and of gaining full- or part-time employment. However, there are other, less quantifiable, but significant benefits both to the women themselves and to society at large. The women may well gain a deeper insight into their situations and the institutional structures that surround them. They may experience an enhanced sense of freedom and choice, which often leads to more critical questioning, to increased self-respect for their own thoughts and ideas and to greater involvement in community and political life. Some of the young women I worked with are now active in their own groups. They are using the skills they have gained to help the growth and development of others. Occasionally they are doing this through a more structured role as a trainer but their interventions are mainly made through the informal and continuing process of offering support and encouragement. Others have tested out their new perceptions and attitudes through travel abroad and through an enlarged engagement with other cultures.

A key element of the processes which I have been discussing here is the recognition of existing skills and interests, and the development of these in activities which are not only transferable, but are recognized and valued in the world outside the young women's daily experience. This development can be seen in individual histories: one young women developed her typing into an interest in computing; another who enjoyed netball undertook a sports leadershp course, coming back into the local playscheme as a playleader; and another's courage resulted in her poetry being published in a major anthology of young women's writing. It can also be seen in the movement from shared activity to collective projects. For example, young women in a local youth club experimented with role play and drama, went on to involvement in a city-wide film on anti-sexism. In another case musical improvization sessions led to a small group building their own sound system. In yet another instance, learning rock-climbing skills enabled two or three groups of young women to open International Women's Day by abseiling down the clock tower of the Town Hall.

Community workers need to be clear sighted and be conscious of possibilities and constraints. Their role is to encourage people to recognize what exists, to help people see what might be achievable and to enable them to find the means to get there. The challenge for community workers is to understand and make visible those mechanisms and opportunities which will enable marginalized and disadvantaged groups to enhance their own personal, social and political power.

CHAPTER 5

Informal education: a place in the new school curriculum?

DAVID BURLEY

Teachers' perceptions of informal education vary greatly. There are those who have a developed view of the contribution of informal methods and contexts to curriculum development; others view their prime purpose as teaching a subject and perceive informal methods as marginal. Finally there are many who are active in extra-curricular activities but who opt not to apply that experience within other curriculum areas. Informal education offers schools the opportunity to inject more relevance than is possible within the existing formal curriculum. For example, Thomas argues that teachers in the pastoral system are better placed than any of their colleagues to understand the dissatisfaction some students feel with existing curriculum provision:

> The reason for suggesting the 'pastoral' area as a likely starting point for these initiatives (to combat dissatisfaction) is the change already taking place in this area. Particularly through the use of prepared material in form periods. These activities are outside the formal curriculum and need not be bound by some of its familiar constraints. Indeed, in some respects where personal skills programmes emphasise independence of judgement and co-operativeness they are already engaged in making parts of the schools 'hidden' curriculum more open and explicit which is an important first step in challenging practice in the more formal curriculum.
>
> Thomas 1985: 178–9

In general, informal education in schools tends to be underplayed. Given the supremacy of the examination system and, more recently, the rise of the National Curriculum, informal education is found in pockets of activity rather than in explicit policy. However, the term is used to describe different aspects of secondary schooling.

- Through the pastoral and welfare system teachers can take a personal interest in students' general well-being and foster home–school links, as well as being in charge of tutor groups.
- Students may opt for modular courses which are not examinable. Teachers may use these sessions as opportunities to share personal interests using informal methods. Examples might include making a video, producing a community newssheet, improving or learning a new sport, community involvement.
- Schools' councils offer students in some schools opportunities to organize social events or debate issues concerning the running of the school; in some cases they can gain access to agreed areas of decision making on the way in which the school is run.
- Much of the curriculum innovation through TVEI and CPVE incorporates informal education aims and methods of developing the personal and social competence required for adult life.
- Residential work can be a component of coursework within several areas of the formal curriculum, including pre-vocational work. Within this setting informal education is extensively used.
- A large number of schools offer lunch-time clubs and after-school activities which range from the small scale, involving a single member of staff, to activities such as drama and music productions supported by several teachers.
- Many schools have youth wings attached or in close proximity. These often have joint community tutor/leader teacher appointments. The worker may make inputs into the school to support informal education and develop youth provision. This may include residential work and support for disaffected students.
- Informal education is frequently used as a way of working with students with special learning needs.

Several things need saying here. Some of these activities fall outside the scope of informal education as it is discussed in the opening chapters. However, they can be placed alongside the traditions of practice described as informal within primary schooling. When approaching such work we need to be clear about the basis upon which it has been defined. Different practitioners are drawn to the same activity with varying aims and objectives. Involvement in informal education by students and staff often flows from a desire to compensate for limitations in the content or methodology of the formal curriculum. Many would argue it is a way of positively enhancing that curriculum. It is evident from the examples of informal education given here that it is not generally associated with courses which are externally examined. Yet this distinction has become increasingly blurred with emerging systems of self-assessment and profiling. Students are at liberty to include a range of experiences gained through informal education – not necessarily school-related – within their personal profiles. These may be produced for job interviews. There are obvious dangers that the motives for participating in such activities will be increasingly related to credentialling and validation. Schools could become seduced into producing impressive ranges of extra-curricular activities and optional courses. These might be published in school prospectuses or participation might be expected by potential employers. This emphasis may come to constrain the responsiveness of informal educators to individual learning needs. Under local management of schools, institutions may choose, or be obliged, to offer activities which bring financial reward to the school, with those who are unable to pay being further disadvantaged. In this extreme form, what is labelled as informal education could become as formalized as some other aspects of the curriculum.

The attractions and distractions of informal education

For many teachers informal education complements their work by offering opportunities for getting to know students better and for working with students of different ages across curriculum boundaries. Some see this as a vital extension of their pastoral role. Many view informal education as a way of gaining greater fulfilment in their jobs, as a chance to share their interests with students, to engage in joint activity with colleagues and to work with other agencies.

Students are attracted to informal education because it provides them with an opportunity to feel recognized for their own worth in settings in which students can influence and control the pace, as well as the content, of their learning. Many feel that they can contribute in these settings in their own way: that they are valued for what they have to contribute and feel a greater ownership of the learning experience. Informal education can offer students a chance to try out new things, to take risks and extend their experience beyond the immediate environment of the school. It can act as a catalyst where it is a departure from more routine experiences.

When informal education appears within the mainstream curriculum the response of students will be varied. Some will immediately identify with the methods, while others will feel it is a distraction from the pursuit of examination subjects or their core curriculum. Some pupils have great difficulty in coping with the transitions involved in moving from a formal to an informal approach and confusion can block their ability to take part. A particular problem here can be pupils' association of teachers with some of the more controlling and authoritarian aspects of the classroom. Certain kinds of informal education may actually be perceived by students as primarily punitive or a control mechanism: A way of keeping them quiet, or of sustaining their commitment, however limited, to schooling. Students responses to informal education bear no consistent relationship to their academic ability. The key distinguishing factor, however, is the degree and nature of choice which students have over participation, and the quality of relationships developed with staff. If informal education within the curriculum is given a low status by some students then there is no doubt a connection between this and the priorities and resources given to it by staff. As with formal learning, it will tend to have meaning within an institution such as a school only when it has a perceived and explicit relevance.

For many teachers informal education is an essential element of their work. Others may wish their role to be more narrowly defined:

> Schools are concerned with the educational development of children. The proper job of the teacher is to teach. It is dangerous for teachers to get involved in meeting the social and other needs of children and in any case they do not have time. The sole purpose of pastoral care and the promotion of good home school relations is to enable children to have access to education.
>
> Welton 1985: 61

Welton proceeds to reflect upon the view that many teachers are anxious to limit their pastoral role; for some this will assume a very low priority when set alongside other demands. It is legitimate to feel there must be limitations to a teacher's role. In contrast, there are a substantial number who view the pastoral system and informal education as critical to their practice. How can these seemingly different positions be reconciled within the curriculum and life of a school?

The relationship of informal education to the overall aims, practices and curriculum of the school must be defined. Clear policy statements must promote a positive understanding of the contribution it can offer to the life of the school. An analysis of the various elements of informal education which deal with welfare, recreation and social education might be a basis for planning and resource allocation. The contribution of informal method to the formal curriculum should also be considered.

All those with an interest should have an input into policy planning. There is a challenge to schools in the way such policies are constructed. The process of developing a policy provides opportunities for teachers and members of the community, as well as young people, to participate in an informal education process. Such policies should clarify the resource needs of informal education and be accompanied by in-service training for teachers and other educators. Particular areas worthy of attention are personal and social education, participation and decision making by young people, counselling, guidance and support. The development of informal education policies in schools might do much to help clarify curriculum areas, job descriptions of staff, posts of special responsibility and the organization and support of the work. More explicit informal education policy can provide a framework within which a greater range of resources from within the school and from outside can be tapped and developed. However, the difficulties of achieving this should not be underestimated.

The role of informal education can often get lost in the pressures and dynamics of many of the institutions and systems in which educators operate. It is difficult to create the time to meet colleagues and reflect upon the learning which has taken place. Teachers often work in isolation. For informal education to make an effective contribution to the life of a school, and to benefit individual students, opportunities must be provided for teachers and others involved in it to reflect and analyse and for the result to be fed back to future practice. Periods of reflection and evaluation also provide important opportunities for others to find a role for themselves within the school's informal curriculum, so creating a structural link between teachers, parents, and personnel from other agencies. This would help youth workers, for example, when they were attached to schools. The cohabitation of youth workers and teachers in many school settings is an example where structural relationships are assumed to exist but do not necessarily imply a shared understanding. The youth worker can be drawn into remedial activity, dealing with symptoms rather than identifying causes and can be badly positioned to influence change.

Change in schools is currently taking place at two key levels: one in relation to the curriculum, the other, regarding the form of financial and management control. Both have implications for informal education. The National Curriculum inevitably means that less time will be available for teaching staff to participate in informal education within school hours. Changes in management and financial control will also have an impact on the extent to which informal education can develop in schools and in association with them.

Curriculum

There has been a substantial rethinking of the examination system in recent years and a more rigorous pursuit of outcome goals in education. In part this has been associated with an increased concern with skills and the new vocationalism. This shift in emphasis has a particular impact upon informal education, where it is process and not outcome that is generally important. Activities take on the cloak of informality which conceals tight behavioural objectives. Informal situations might be used to enable young people to gain certain social skills. When they demonstrated these skills they would presumably have completed the process. It is perhaps best not to think of this as informal education. Informal situations do not *per se* constitute informal education. The opening chapter of this book argued that tight outcome goals were incompatible with informal pedagogy.

   While many of the current developments may not be classed as informal education, they do utilize a number of elements which run parallel with certain familiar concerns. Teachers within the GCSE structure are central to the assessment process, while the development of student self-assessment has the potential to encourage students to take more responsibility for their own learning. Curriculum innovations, such as TVEI, supposedly emphasize 'sound preparation for life in a technological society both in work and leisure' and encourage methods which are well known to informal educators, such as 'alternative learning strategies based on active participation including work experience and residential experience' (DES 1987b: 2). TVEI has attracted the interest of staff and students, encouraging an appetite for new approaches to learning. Within TVEI students are:

> offered a core experience in tutorial time which includes units of work on careers education, study skills, group projects, work experience and management shadowing. There are also two core modules chosen from IT or business studies, and political awareness or performing arts.
>
> DES 1987b: 4

I am not suggesting that TVEI or CPVE are synonymous with informal education: they are not. But, together with other developments, such as GCSE, they indicate the potential within some parts of the curriculum to restructure learning methods and styles, as well as relationships between students and teachers. It would be surprising if the start which has now been made does not lead in the longer term to a more radical investigation of the organization and purpose of schooling. TVEI, CPVE and other curriculum innovations, have enabled and encouraged teaching staff to spend time out of schools on an unprecedented scale. Ideas and new perspectives have been shared with colleagues and there has been extended contact with industry and other sectors. Initiatives such as TVEI have involved schools in using outside funding, both time limited and focused. The benefits of this should not be underestimated: it is one of a number of mechanisms which are helping to open up schools and broaden their contact with other agencies; schools are becoming less insular.

The introduction of the National Curriculum will have an inevitable impact on the place of informal education in schools. The National Curriculum covers three core subjects (mathematics, English and science) and seven foundation subjects (history, geography, a modern foreign language, music, physical education and technology). Those which are not explicitly included within the core and foundation subjects are expected to be fitted into the limited 'minority time'. Some fear that this curriculum will lead to some subjects being viewed as optional extras which may survive only if parents are willing or able to pay.

The implementation of the National Curriculum must inevitably direct the attention of schools to securing student competence in given areas, particularly in core subjects. This will encourage schools to concentrate resources and time still further upon the examinable areas at the expense of what may be regarded by some as nonessential. The criteria by which schools may be judged as 'good' suggest that participation in extra-curricular activity is a significant benchmark. There are inherent contradictions between these two positions. The onus is on schools to clarify their own policies towards extra-curricular activity as well as the small part of the school day which is designated as available for other than the core and foundation subjects.

While it must be hoped that schools can continue to offer a varied curriculum within the national framework, it may well be that it is the quality of teaching (and use of more informal means) that will differentiate the 'good' school from the 'bad'. An alternative response might be for a school to recognize the importance and value of informal education but plan to deal with it outside the framework of the formal curriculum. This approach could frustrate the development of many of the links between the formal and informal pedagogy discussed in this chapter, especially where it is some other body such as the Youth Service or separate community education service which is seen as responsible for such provision. There are many examples on the continent of separate informal education provision at the end of the formal school day. While this might ensure a positive place for informal education at a time when it is in danger of being given a low priority, it does hamper a holistic understanding of the school.

Management and financial control

The National Curriculum is an integral part of a package of reforms designed to shift responsibility for schools from local authorities to individual institutions and central government. Complementary to this discussion is the implementation of those clauses of the 1986 Education Act which give more powers to parents and governors, alongside heads, for the management of the curriculum. In conjunction with this schools are now obliged to develop schemes of local financial management (LFM). Individual institutions are required to control their own finances based on a single budget administered through the LEA. The budget covers all aspects of running a school. Under LFM the governing bodies are also responsible for the appointments of all staff. Within these arrangements schools will have greater flexibility to determine how they raise and allocate funds. This includes accruing the benefits from letting where dual use of premises takes place, as with adult education and community groups.

Schools are being encouraged, and given incentives, to enter a commercial market in which they will be expected to compete with one another and to generate revenue over and above what they get from statutory sources. Given the requirements of the National Curriculum it is increasingly likely that these funds will be used (as they are already to varying degrees in most schools) to support the formal curriculum. In such circumstances informal education could be subjected to new pressures. It could, as is currently the case in some schools, be used as a means of income generation to support the prescribed curriculum. Schools could become partially dependent on financially lucrative leisure-directed services to support their legal obligations. The payment of teachers' salaries and incentive allowances could increasingly be identified with income generation. Under these conditions informal education would be leisure- and consumer-oriented and valued for its financial rather than educational contribution. Another view might be that LFM, and hence the determination of staff salaries at the school level, could possibly place even greater pressure on staff to engage in informal education as a route to promotion and increased salary. This could be enforced as a condition of their contracts, as it is in the USA.

Some schools are extending the logic of LFM into opting out of local authority control altogether. Headteachers and others are being required to consider more rigorously how the schools in which they work are promoted to parents, to students, the community and industry. With falling rolls and covert pressure for selection, few working within the education system would deny that an environment of competition now exists. The nature and focus of accountability is also changing. On the one hand, it can be argued, the movement away from local authority control in favour of governing bodies and headteachers represents increased local autonomy. Equally, the trend epitomized by such developments as the National Curriculum may be taken as indicative of movement in the opposite direction towards the centre, leaving schools as agents of central government policy. In other words, the rhetoric may belie reality. This tension is reflected in two conflicting perspectives within community education. Foreman (1987: 2) argues that:

> Governing bodies are also being forced to play a much more active role. Political appointments will be fewer as parents along with teachers and co-opted members become the majority. Alert schools will ensure wide representation from the community. Governors must now report to parents on their stewardship.

In contrast, Richards (1986: 2) maintains of central government that:

> The intention quite clearly is not to offer more choice, but to exercise greater control over the workings of teachers and schools, through finance, market forces and curriculum demands. I suggest these initiatives have nothing to do with the principles of community education. Quite the reverse, they are designed to promote a subject centred approach, and it denies any attempt to develop a learner centred one.

The impact of all this upon community education initiatives, and various elements of informal education provision placed within schools, but not necessarily funded or managed through main-line budgets, such as youth work, remains unclear. There has been a move in many authorities to separate youth work more clearly from school or college funding in order to retain direct local authority control over budgets and staff. It should additionally be noted that LFM has obvious contractual implications for youth workers and community educators who are employed in schools.

The relationship of informal education to secondary schooling

At this point it is helpful to clarify a number of key questions regarding the relationship of informal education to secondary schooling. When does formal education end and informal begin? How much does the compulsory nature of schooling until 16 affect methods, styles and intentions of informal learning? How is informal learning in schools identified and how is it linked with other workers and agencies such as the Youth Service? What effect does a commitment to informal learning have on a school's relationships with other bodies?

All these questions relate to the ways in which informal education in schools is perceived. The new curriculum innovations, such as TVEI, CPVE and GCSE, have led to a more critical appraisal of what is taught in schools. These innovations have affected the methods used, the nature of relationships between staff, students and, in some cases, parents, members of the community and industry. Experiential learning has the potential to engage students, teachers, and members of the community in some shared learning and interaction within the remit of the formal curriculum. As such methods develop and become integrated within the curriculum, there is at least the potential for the erosion of the barriers between informal and formal approaches. Some teachers' roles could theoretically change from concentrating on the dissemination of knowledge to a more centrally acknowledged role of organizing learning experience identified in dialogue with students and other relevant parties. This would, in practice, bring teachers closer to the role and orientation of colleagues in other parts of the education service, and for that matter, with many people in industry and the voluntary sector who have an educational and developmental role. It need not be assumed that this learning will always take place within a school building. Greater commonality of role and function across schooling and other agencies has the potential for developing new alliances and allegiances and, consequently, more varied learning settings and styles.

The implication here is that unless teachers, heads, and governing bodies understand and appreciate the need for informal education and recognize examples of good practice within their own institutions, no amount of instrumentalism from outside can effect enduring change. Good informal education practice should encourage students to learn directly from their experiences and offer space for reflection and review. Residential experiences, work experience schemes and community involvement opportunities cannot be ends in themselves; they are material on which new learning can be built. Within them there may be both formal and informal opportunities for students to reflect and review as well as plan. One formal development in this respect, has been the framing of criteria for records of student achievement. This has been a significant step in spelling out learning objectives within schooling. While these records are something of an anathema to process-focused informal educators, one benefit is that their use in individual subject areas can lead to increasing debate about cross-curricular competences. The more this happens the more education will move from the traditionally-orientated acquisition of information to skills acquisition. One significant outcome of the use of student profiles, for example, is that they can lead to greater student autonomy in the student–teacher relationship. The Northamptonshire 14–16 Project was able to report (1987: 10):

> At school level records of achievement are being logged by pupils and staff in consultation. Initially these discussions tended to be dominated by the teacher, but there are reports that pupils are now beginning to be more active in discussions and genuine negotiation is beginning to occur.

It would be misleading to suggest there has been a revolution in all schools; but there is movement and it is one which informal educators should note. The significant thing about the change is that key aspects are generated from within the secondary schooling system itself. Discussion of change is being conducted in a language which teachers have chosen to adopt and feel they can apply. It may be worth comparing this with attempts to integrate aspects of youth work into schools, directly or in association with them. A degree of tolerance may well exist between services and workers; but this seldom gives rise to integrated work, a view echoed in a LEA community education review (Clayton 1987: 22) which noted that:

> The language used by community educators to describe their educational perspective is frustrating to principals and indeed to day school staff trained and experienced in work undertaken in more structured learning environments. Furthermore 'outreach work' and 'networking' are notions which hard pressed principals and teachers have little time to explore. They want more immediate and practical outcomes from community education staff. One principal commented 'we have a long way to go to develop mutual understanding'.

It is clearly difficult to develop informal education policies and processes within schools and colleges in a way which makes sense to teachers and managers, particularly as the language and apparent form of some of the new formal initiatives mirror some aspects of informal pedagogy, but often have a very different starting point. The more the skills associated with informal education are openly acknowledged as being shared by both teachers and other practitioners, the more chance there is of dialogue between exponents of the different approaches and the possibility of a common purpose and language. However, major problems remain, especially with regard to differing orientations to product and process. Where formal educators have begun to approach the curriculum through a process perspective, the basis for a shared understanding with informal educators is heightened. On the other hand, those who are orientated to product and the setting of tight objectives for the learner, will, no doubt, remain unmoved by the claims of informal education.

Informal education through community education

Community schools and colleges have to varying degrees already gone some way towards reconciling the differing educational traditions of formal schooling, youth and community work and adult education, providing mechanisms by which informal education can be expanded and developed. Many community schools remain little more than dual-use institutions; yet there has always been a strong move towards an integrated institution which acknowledges 'that education is in the business of contriving that people form their value systems and learn the art of social involvement in the shared common predicament' (Toogood 1980: 162).

Leicestershire, among a number of LEAS, has tried to institutionalize ways in which the limitations of the dual-establishment can be reduced by attempts to widen the number of teachers engaged in community activities. In five of their community colleges the community teacher scheme has been introduced. Secondary teachers were contracted, as an integrated part of their job, to work at evenings, weekends and holidays in educational programmes involving all age ranges (Clayton 1987). There has been a tendency within the scheme for teachers to find themselves as potential part-time community workers without appropriate training and support. Teachers have not always naturally gravitated towards youth work and many indicate that they encounter difficulty in giving their '10 per cent' the priority it deserves. Schools have found it hard to identify and maintain appropriate structures through which work can be supported. Development work undertaken on the basis of approximately half a day a week is likely to achieve only limited results. There is variation across colleges in how the work is organized but generally teams cover areas such as youth work, sports and recreation, continuing education, parent support and new projects. While one college has appointed a full-time trainer to support and develop the community teacher scheme, and another has made a part-time appointment, there is a general feeling that not enough priority has been given to looking at the support needs of teachers or how the extended role fits in with their mainstream work.

Experience of working with community teachers indicates that there is only a limited value in expecting teaching staff to dip into work that remains outside their predominant training and orientation. It is far better to assist them to do the job they are already engaged upon and help them to extend it, or look at it in a different way, rather than adding on alternative activities. It is prudent for those wishing to develop informal education to find ways of making it more central to the curriculum and culture of the schools. It is inappropriate to rely on goodwill alone. This would marginalize the work at a time when it requires a higher profile. The developments mentioned in this chapter refer to starting points for informal education which begin with the experience of the school and which, for example, youth and community workers might wish to engage in.

Conclusion

Informal education exists in schools whether or not it is openly recognized by the staff, students and parents who use them. At present it is a diverse process with varying aims and objectives and a variety of intentions and contexts, but arguably offering a common purpose: that of self-development. The benefits of informal education are felt to be more participation, choice, independence and a sense of fulfilment for students and staff alike: a recognition of ownership of their learning and work.

The current period of financial and curriculum change has coincided with a time when education itself is changing from within. We may be at a watershed in terms of the possible future of schooling and hence not only of the place of informal education within it but also of the relationships of others, not least youth workers and the Youth Service, with the school. Within the school those with a concern for informal education are increasingly adopting similar methods of intervention, which involve negotiated learning, group work, guidance, counselling and support and the promotion of skills in cooperation and problem solving. Roles include being a facilitator and an organizer of learning experiences and require the educator to adopt the role of resource person. This experience is complemented within the formal arena. TVEI has provided opportunities for teachers to adopt some of the roles of informal educators, a significant departure from the traditional role of the classroom teacher. However, it is a matter of some urgency that staff agree on those elements of informal education which they wish to develop more centrally within the curriculum and culture of the school.

There needs to be a more open and explicit advocacy of the contribution informal pedagogy makes within the school. This should provide a firmer basis for other informal educators to become involved in and associated with the school. The relationship of the school with its community will, therefore, be critical; this relationship will increasingly legitimate a school's philosophy and activities. The school's ability to reflect local interests will depend on the nature of the dialogue between local people and the school. A school's policy on informal learning should be an important contributory factor in determining the quality of that dialogue. The informal dimension of the curriculum could thus assume a high profile in the eyes of parents and others, not least young people, when they select the appropriate school.

CHAPTER 6

Neighbourhood, crime and informal education

DEBBIE SADDINGTON

The Probation Service has experienced a shift in emphasis from 'first aid' to 'preventative' work. This effectively provides the framework for involvement in community-based practice and community education at a grass roots level. It also contributes to the wide development of informal and social educational networks, whether explicitly structured or not, within severely disadvantaged communities. The primary objective of such involvement derives from an emphasis upon the need for 'effective' and 'realistic' crime prevention and reduction strategies. At the same time there is often a desire to achieve long-term qualitative improvements in the lives and circumstances of individual clients and their families.

The new focus

As Stern (1987) suggests, several strands in thinking about criminal justice have come together to produce the new focus, generally referred to as crime prevention and reduction. These entail both community participation and ultimately some form of education. Initially, for example, there is growing recognition that controlling crime in a community is separate and distinct from the process of apprehending and dealing with individual offenders. As the Lord Chief Justice put it:

> Neither Police nor Courts nor prison can solve the problem of the 'rising' crime rate. By the time that the criminal falls into the hands of the police, and more particularly, by the time he reaches Court, it is too late. The damage has been done. The remedy, if it can be found, must be sought a great deal earlier.
>
> quoted Stern 1987: 209

Debbie Saddington

Movement towards a more community-orientated crime prevention model has widespread appeal. Stern maintains that one facet of
this shift is a diversion of research interest away from individual
offenders and how they are dealt with towards a concern with
analysing crime as a phenomenon. This encourages a wider and
more constructive overview by looking beyond largely uninforma-
tive crime statistics, to crime as experienced by individuals and
communities and the nature of those communities in which it is most
prevalent and from which the majority of offenders derive. Broad
(1985) argues that the current trend towards community-based
probation projects reflects a shift away from theories encompassing
individual pathology towards a wider interactionist approach. The
argument is further developed by the assertion by some that,
theoretically, both community and probation work can be seen as
having the same aims: a concern with effecting improvements in
the quality of individual and family lives. However, Broad maintains that mainstream community work differs from what the
Probation Service provides in its emphasis on social change
achieved by collective action and campaigning. The Probation
Service's emphasis, in contrast, is on personal change achieved via
individualized casework.

Probation involvement in community work can be interpreted
as a movement away from rigid adherence to the individual/
pathological model of orientation. This model has an implicit
emphasis upon Social Darwinism and overwhelmingly concentrates
on individual inadequacies and individual deviance. The movement
has been towards a more structural explanation of crime and delin-
quency, which places greater emphasis on social and economic
inequalities and constraints as contributors to criminal activity. In
support of this Bottoms and McWilliams (1979) argue that as crime
is predominantly social, so any crime reduction strategy must be
socially based, requiring community involvement.

Although treatment strategies as applied to communities are
inappropriate for crime prevention, important change can be
effected by taking into account microstructural and social
integration factors.

Microstructural factors comprise 'those features of the local situation
which appear to be crime producing and on which local residents
may have some influence' (*ibid*: 191). These include housing policy,
employment and educational opportunities, recreational facilities,
youth provision, police relations and environmental improvements.

Social integration is based upon the proposition that other things being equal, 'communities with strongly cohesive bonds tend to produce less crime' (*ibid*: 191–2).

The primary purpose of introducing of such concepts is to illustrate the way in which the collective working and interagency approach of statutory and voluntary agencies, various groups and local people in extremely deprived and alienated communities can gradually attempt to at least alleviate certain extreme situations of hardship and stress. They may simultaneously engender a more coherent and productive community spirit and self-image.

Most of the community work projects within the Probation Service likewise choose a particular geographical entity, focusing on areas brought to their attention because of the high incidence of social and criminal difficulties. One assumption behind this approach can be that people living in the same place have a common sense of belonging and a shared network of activity and community life. This 'community spirit' emphasizes the potential for social cohesiveness and the absence of conflict which will enable the officer to link with and work alongside local people to achieve change and improvements (NAPO 1984–5: 1).

Neighbourhood-based informal education in practice

The educative nature of such community-based projects, particularly those which use concentrated and targeted group work and involve community initiatives and liaison, becomes apparent. The main aspects of such an 'educative' process can be defined as:

- helping people to identify needs and to come together as a group;
- helping groups achieve their goals; and
- encouraging people to work collectively on problems.

When I was working in an extremely deprived council estate in Newcastle, I concentrated on work in two areas to achieve these aims. The first was intensive group development work. This is an essential prerequisite to achieving long-term change and focuses on specific 'target' groups, i.e. women, young people, the young unemployed. Within such a context community work and informal education become inseparable, the mechanism of the group allowing for the provision of much needed social and recreational opportunities. Such a group additionally offers limited alleviation of various stresses and anxieties and allows for the direct establishment of a rapport, identification and understanding with the local people involved. In effect, the educative process becomes two-way. Mutual sharing and the exchange of ideas and views take place within a largely unstructured, informal and relaxed atmosphere. However, the importance of activity-based work must not be undervalued. This allows for the development of a more cohesive group basis before tackling more explicitly structured issues and project-based work (i.e. political and social awareness, anti-sexist and anti-racist work, health education). However, the validity of activity based work is also acknowledged as a legitimate area of concentration in its own right, given its stimulus to overall personal and group development and expression. Equally it can emphasize the importance of collective working and decision making, self-awareness and belief in individual and group abilities and potential.

Involvement in wider community development and interagency work is required in an attempt to realistically increase and improve the quality of life within deprived communities. Such involvement requires wholesale local support and cooperation. Group work initially ameliorates certain immediate difficulties for those involved directly within a group. But these are generally on a relatively superficial, limited and symptomatic level, other courses of action are required to pressure for change at a higher and more effective level by tackling structures.

Group work often provides a platform from which local people may gain the confidence and assertiveness to become more actively involved in campaigning for change and neighbourhood improvements. Community education enacted via group and wider development work is, therefore, an essential mechanism by which local people are encouraged to become aware of the control they can exert over particular aspects of their own lives and the change in social conditions which can be achieved by collective action.

The two-way educational process referred to earlier is again highlighted. By locating directly within the heart of a neighbourhood a greater appreciation of the primary areas of need can be developed in conjunction with the local people involved. This contributes to the more effective targeting of available resources and, ultimately, improvements in service delivery, via coordination of community planning and liaison. Clearly There is a danger of using relatively grand terms for fairly small-scale projects. However, taken as a whole a number of agencies and groups working together, within a neighbourhood, can have quite a significant effect, though this is not necessarily always tangible.

The increased understanding of the context of offending which community-based practice gives may also enhance service delivery and ultimately reduce crime. Simultaneously, it may lead to the amelioration of certain crime-producing factors. Effectively, only practical experience at a direct grass roots level can engender an understanding of the conditions and environmental circumstances which manipulate and influence individual and group behaviour. Given the nature of areas of severe disadvantage and alienation it is generally essential that group work involves both probation clients and non-clients. Such a focus is an imperative if truly 'preventative' work is to take place. There is, therefore, a need to overcome the general perception that probation projects are, or should be, solely client-orientated.

Aspects of locally based informal education

A crucial element of effective education is an in-depth appreciation of the social and cultural life of a community. Without acknowledging and taking such factors into account, group and wider community development work is ultimately doomed to failure and rejection. Within communities, different subcultures and value systems are found. In certain localities a criminal subculture may exist – an ultimate acceptance of the legitimacy of crime, particularly in relation to theft and burglary. Not everyone in the local community holds or condones such attitudes. However, the necessity of committing offences may be seen by many community members, in my experience, as essential not only to supplement income but also as a means of acquiring individual status and reducing boredom. This can engender a deterministic and fatalistic attitude. Many individuals see themselves as occupational and educational 'failures', who will inevitably end up in prison or young offenders' institutions. Life is seen as consisting primarily of blocked opportunities and conflict.

Attitudes to education mirror this fatalism, although this is hardly surprising given the overall negative experiences most have encountered within the formal educational process. We are not highlighting individual and social group inadequacy here but pointing out that such attitudes and experience are predominantly the result of wider structural factors. It is against such a background and overwhelming odds that informal education most often takes place. Any change in attitudes and behaviour achieved can therefore be accomplished only gradually and is often marginal.

The personality of the worker

Challenging entrenched attitudes and value bases is achieved not only via group work but often indirectly during the course of a seemingly unrelated activity, a casual conversation or within the context of a general group get together. In this process a number of factors are of considerable importance. As Foreman has suggested elsewhere in this volume, the personality of the project worker(s) is of considerable significance. Local people often identify initially with personalities rather than principles. The value stance of workers, their flexibility and ability to handle autonomy will have a particular impact upon those they work with. These in themselves may make or break a piece of work. However, other factors are equally relevant. Newcomb (1961) indicated that people will tend to be attracted to others if they believe that the others have values and attitudes similar to their own. From my own experience this has been particularly the case when the worker has displayed a fair degree of partisanship, empathy and personal support for group and individual experiences. The perception by group members that a worker may come from a situation similar to their own (e.g. social class background) can also enhance the development of a constructive relationship. Patterns of speech are a further factor: use of neighbourhood language and terminology may on occasions be productive. However, over-assimilation and identification can lead to ineffectiveness. There is always a danger of workers becoming, or remaining, engulfed within common-sense understandings and emotional commitments. To be able to contribute to the well-being of those that they are working with it is necessary for them to infuse their practice with a critical reflectiveness. In other words, workers have to strive to be both in the situation and outside it. This is not to denigrate commitment to, and identity with, a particular group or neighbourhood. Rather, it is to say that such commitment and identity should always remain open to critical assessment.

The significance of personality raises important questions about how workers are educated. Formalized education and training for community and social work may not produce effective informal educators. Many of the elements required for effective working within informal education can appear to be instinctive and intuitive. Particular personality traits can be as significant as learnt behaviour. These include the ability to make people feel at ease, relaxed, comfortable and to create non-threatening situations. Sensitivity, tolerance and the ability to assess group dynamics and defuse aggression and tension, are further factors, as well as a high degree of commitment and personal motivation. Having said this, we should not fall into the trap of dismissing education and training. Reflection on self and practice can bring about major changes in the way in which workers understand themselves and their work. However, this does demand a rather different orientation in training and education.

Understanding groups

Worker acceptance in an area is a vital corollary to project success, while to avoid alienation group work must be properly paced and evaluated. More explicitly structured group working is unrealistic given the general resource and staffing constraints placed upon many community-based projects and the sheer size and scale of the problems to be tackled. It is imperative to set objectives at an achievable level, both in terms of the project worker and the groups being catered for. It is important to avoid creating false expectations and aspirations which would result in frustration, disaffection and subsequent reduction of confidence. This applies to workers, group members and project users.

Informal education, when enacted through the mechanism of the group, implies direct face-to-face work with specific territorial groups; that is, individuals from a predefined physical locality. The nature of the groups targeted is primarily dependent upon the particular social agency involved and the remit, skills, experience and resources of the worker and project concerned. A great deal of ambiguity surrounds the general term group work. In order to clarify its meaning within the context of the above discussion, reference is made here to E. J. Thomas's work (1967). The orientation and methodology adopted are highly dependent upon the ideological overview held by the particular agency involved and the individual disposition of the project worker. Different models and approaches to group work reflect divergent theoretical and political positions, ranging from an emphasis upon individual change to concentration upon structural intervention through collective action. Brown (1979: 5) highlights the above point by utilizing a definition of the function of the group made by Konopka (1963), who maintained that:

> Social group work is a method of social work which helps individuals to enhance their social functioning through purposeful

group experiences and to cope more effectively with their personal, group or community problems.

Such an emphasis is traditionalist and concentrates upon change within the individual, the significance of social roles and only implicitly on social dysfunctioning. The view adopted here goes beyond simply helping an individual with a problem. It places greater significance upon:

> action and influence as well as reaction and adaption. The definition becomes more comprehensive if we add: groupwork provides a context in which *individuals help each other*; it is a method of *helping groups* as well as helping individuals; and it can enable individuals and groups to *influence* and *change* personal, group, organisational and community problems.
>
> Brown 1979: 6, emphasis in original

The groups with which I have worked have been structured to the extent that they all had a membership which shared common experiences, difficulties and interests – be this as young people, offenders, women or unemployed. This has subsequently assisted in the development of a common purpose and intent; the resultant increase in mutual trust and support, led to greater coherence and, ultimately, a higher level of stress success. Some groups have a clearly defined or explicit membership, while in other cases the boundaries between who is and is not a member are somewhat hazy and can alter radically over a short period of time. Indeed, questions about this boundary can play an important, and often positive, part in the work. It is not only the 'internal' dynamics of the group that are important.

By and large the groups discussed here are small, generally with between 3 and 14 participants. Many of these small groups were seen as existing for a particular purpose, however ill defined. Within my experience this has tended to involve confidence and assertiveness building, both individual and collective. Further functions of the group may relate to problem solving, such as the resolving of immediate difficulties with accommodation, relationships or financial worries. The group may, more straightforwardly, act as a basis for developing social networks or recreational opportunities which would otherwise be limited or non-existent. Community-based groups incorporate several aspects.

The groups with which I have had experience, were often difficult to place in specific categories as they incorporated elements from a variety of models. This was particularly so when a number of ideological stances were involved. In this instance, an organization, the Probation Service, which, as a result of its historical and practical origins is rooted predominantly in an individualistic and remedial interpretation of social and group difficulties, is set besides my own position as a worker and the project ethos. This sees wider societal factors as more significant in producing social problems and the resultant behavioural patterns than the former.

Workers, agencies and neighbourhoods

The policy context and orientation of a project will frequently have been established before a particular worker arrives. The degree to which workers are able to influence a particular context is especially dependent upon the level of autonomy accorded to them. Value neutrality is a misnomer in group work, and this equally applies to the functioning of the worker. Each personal action and spoken word reflects a particular stance and value base, which will inevitably have some impact upon the orientation of the group, its aims and how the group perceives the worker. The success or otherwise of the group and the informal educative process as a whole is ultimately linked to these factors.

A further area of critical importance is the negotiation of the project and the worker's role within a community. Linked to such negotiation is the central question of local resident acceptance of an agency's involvement within community issues. This is particularly pertinent with an agency such as the Probation Service.

> It is more important than ever that we maintain our commitment to the values of avoiding interference in other people's lives except where it is essential. Workers need to acknowledge that dilemmas and tensions are likely to occur if they shift the emphasis of their work into politically sensitive areas. The difficulties are not merely confined to the workers. Many community members will have searching questions about why they, who may well never have had any involvement with the Courts, should be involved with the Probation Service. The negotiation of one's role in a community can be as difficult as the negotiation within one's own management.
>
> Drakeford 1983: 15

Within informal education it is essential to have explicitly stated objectives, even if these are loosely defined and extremely broad. Objectives may involve articulating issues such as:

- Why is the Probation Service involved in the community work sphere?
- Which elements of a neighbourhood's population are to be targeted?
- Which issues and subjects are to be tackled within the context of the group?
- Resource availability and limitation in terms of staffing, space, specialist training, financial and material factors, and the degree of autonomy available.

Further issues arise when an attempt is made to define the aims of informal education in a neighbourhood context. For example, whose aims are effectively adopted where several protagonists are involved: those of the worker, the individual agency(s), the group members or the community? Conflict over aims may also arise not only between the worker and group members but also between the worker and agency. Again this relates back to ideological position and value base. Any one of these will produce different perceptions of, and proposed solutions to, particular problems and situations. For example, with Probation the view may dominate, on an organizational level, that group work, and ultimately informal education within a community context, should be geared towards change in delinquent and anti-social behaviour. Here the desired outcome will be to produce law-abiding and socially responsible citizens. Ideologically such a view is criminological in origin. Within extremely disadvantaged neighbourhoods such objectives would effectively require emphasis upon deference, subordination and subservience – an acceptance of an individual's, family's or community's 'lot'. The criminological perspective is, therefore, highly individualistic and in many respects inappropriate for community-based working and the effecting of wide-ranging qualitative improvements. The worker, in comparison, may not only want to emphasize the development of the individual within collective situations but also be oriented towards certain collective outcomes.

The nature of programmes

As previously stated, the groups with which I have been involved have incorporated elements of both the individualistic and collective models. Working with women and an unemployed group has not only involved analysing issues such as offending behaviour but also examining issues such as social inequality, discrimination and social group positions. Within such group work emphasis has been placed to a greater or lesser extent upon person-centred and developmental goals. These attempt to encourage individuals to analyse critically, and respond creatively, to their circumstances and experiences.

The mechanisms used to achieve such aims have included role play, the use of guest speakers and group discussions. All have attempted to focus upon individual members' experiences and feelings about such issues as single parenthood, offending, perceptions of their own communities, organizations and institutions which have bearing upon their lives. Group workers play a central role within such sessions, acting as catalysts during the discussion, introducing new topics, supporting group members and suggesting new angles for exploration.

Once a degree of coherence and trust has been established within a group, it has proved constructive to set in train, special projects which highlight particular aspects of members' lives. The client-based women's group referred to earlier, after meeting for a period of nearly two years, undertook a photography project. This aimed to develop particular skills and collective forms of working and to construct, through photographs, views of how the women perceived themselves, their families and circumstances. This led them to analyse the most important factors in their lives, the community within which they lived and the facilities or otherwise which existed. The project also examined intergenerational change within particular group members' families and dominant images of women and motherhood as portrayed in the media, together with the pressures such images bring.

A similar project was undertaken in relation to the young unemployed group and involved several members in painting a mural. The theme was entirely chosen by them. The project allowed the group worker and community artist to spend a considerable time discussing, informally, a range of issues that affected the lives of the group. In several respects the mural itself was actually secondary to the primary objective, which was increased contact and interaction among group members. The mural effectively facilitated discussion with a particularly difficult and disaffected group by deflecting the intensity of the discussion itself. Previous contact with the group had primarily been on an activity basis, outside the project building. Attempts at group discussions within the confines of the community project had been largely unsuccessful before this. However, the art project allowed, for a limited period at least, productive contact with several members of the group for a relatively prolonged period. This produced far stronger personal bonds between individual group

members and the group worker and facilitated honest and constructive discussion of feelings and actions. In this particular group, a
great deal of the discussion focused on offending, because criminal
activity was a central aspect of the lives both of the group members
and other young men on the estate. Discussions subsequently re-
volved around such topics as the need to steal everything in sight and
why members of their own community should be victimized. The
intention of focusing on such issues was to prompt individual
members to take a more considered approach to their actions and
rationalize the likely outcome.

Informal education within the neighbourhood is very different.
The situation is finely balanced and involves compromise, consen-
sus, group and community acceptance and role negotiation. The
worker has to find a place within the environment of the group
members and operate in the context of local socio–cultural factors. In
the community projects which I have been involved with, group
attendance has rarely been compulsory. Individuals attend if they
find that the group is useful and has something to offer. This requires
compromise, consultation and negotiation and loose agreement on
group aims. Although a group in a community setting is not as
organized as it would be in more formal educational surroundings,
some element of structuring is inevitably involved: there have to be
ground rules on group membership, boundaries and other essential
matters. Such structuring allows the worker to operate in a more
coherent, systematic and effective fashion than would otherwise be
possible. Informal education may involve the existence of some
form of contract of agreement, either verbal or written. Ground
rules may cover such issues as:

- making explicit the general or specific aims of the group;
- acknowledging the expectations of individual group members
  and their perception of the group, its purpose and function;
- the basic orientation of the group and its methodology (i.e.
  activities, role play, discussions, games, special projects);
- practical arrangements covering time, place and length of group;
- other conditions (the open or closed nature of group, defined
  membership etc.);
- accepted behaviour (i.e. regular attendance, non-violence, sup-
  portiveness);
- confidentiality.

Openness and honesty are also significant. Group members are
expected to give something of themselves in terms of insights and

feelings. The same can fairly be expected of the worker. However, the degree of self-disclosure must be carefully weighted and aimed at assisting group members to achieve personal and social goals. There have been rather too many examples of workers using such opportunities to explore their own personal concerns and problems with little apparent interest in the requirements of the group. *Appropriate* disclosure can be positive both in its content and in the provision of opportunity for role modelling.

Dilemmas and limitations

At this point it is vitally important to acknowledge, once again, the limitations of informal education and the relatively marginal impact which group and wider community development work has upon the problems being tackled. Objectives must be set at a realistic, achievable level. The terms 'individual and collective consciousness raising and confidence building', for example, would be highly misleading if they implied the wholesale politicization or radicalization of those with whom the informal educator came into contact. More achievable objectives might be to increase individuals' self-belief sufficiently to enable them to make a phone call which involved direct and controlled contact with an 'authority figure'.

After a proper recognition of the limitations of the approach, a further dilemma presents itself. Intervention within a community context can be divided into two main levels. Henderson and Thomas (1987: 35) illustrate this process and product dichotomy.

> A continuing dilemma is whether your interest lies essentially in assisting the self-learning process of individuals through their participation in community groups, or whether it focuses on the achievement of specific tasks which can bring material or psychological benefits to neighbourhoods.

Product models stress the practical gains involved in, for example, tenants' associations, while process models are predominantly concerned with the impact various stages of the process may have on the consciousness, self-esteem and skills of group members themselves. Achieving aims can, of course, lead to further learning, or reinforce existing understandings and skills. However, the informal educator will tend to focus upon process and learning rather than the concrete product. This is not to minimize the significance of product, simply to recognize that the educator is centrally concerned with learning, while the community organizer focuses upon the achievement of concrete gains and facilities for the neighbourhood. This dilemma is very real when the community-based organizer is the Probation Service, which seeks primarily to reduce offending. It can often mean that the worker has to adopt, and somehow reconcile, two different roles – that of educator and organizer. These, in turn, have to be accommodated within that of the Probation Officer.

A further limitation arises from the extent to which informal education and community engagement are tokenistic interventions on the part of the agency. Broad (1985) pinpoints how often 'community' (and subsequently community education) can be used as a 'convenient prefix' to make activities look more humane, desirable and progressive, when in reality such activities lack re-sources, accountability and direction.

In conclusion

The examples offered in this chapter are in many ways not typical. To engage in this kind of practice the Probation Services need to adopt a rather different approach: to restructure roles, to pay atten-tion to terms of entry and objectives and be ready to negotiate. Given the resource constraints and the scale of the problems and situations being faced, it is important to be realistic and acknowledge that any change achieved is generally marginal and piecemeal. Finally, given the inseparable nature of informal education and community-based practice it is essential to perceive the 'educative' process as a mutual one, involving the sharing of ideas and the development of knowl-edge and strategies. Without such an approach any attempt at social change and improvements through the medium of informal edu-cation in the community would probably be doomed to rejection and create further alienation.

CHAPTER 7

Informal education – a Christian perspective

JOHN W. ELLIS

'Can you imagine St Paul being involved with anything like this?' This question came from an ardent Christian as she surveyed our Youth Centre in full swing one evening. To be honest I had to admit I could not. I had a brief mental picture of the great Apostle gathering up his robes the better to line up the cue ball for a shot. But then I could not imagine St Paul climbing into his Ford Escort or dropping in at the local chip shop. It is simply not possible to make that sort of transfer across the centuries. The question had been put in a silly way. The questioner thought that it would highlight the inappropriateness, in Christian terms, of what she saw. Her question, however, had the unfortunate effect of deflecting any serious discussion of the issues involved. Nevertheless these issues need to be addressed.

In the first place there is an assumption that the churches' primary task is educational. Christians are in the business of passing on to others the content of their faith. This assumption is accepted, while at the same time it is recognized that there are Christians who do not see the churches' primary task in these terms.

In the second place there is a question. In what way, if at all, does a youth centre contribute to this primary task? It was her inability to see anything 'educational' happening that led to my friend's rather odd question. She went on to ask whether we had an epilogue – a part of the proceedings when members were given a talk on some aspect of the Christian faith. When I confessed that we did not, I felt myself consigned to the ranks of well intentioned but misguided.

It is this question that we must now explore in some detail. My friend can be forgiven her unease about the whole operation; many who do not share her Christian presuppositions would have equal difficulty in seeing a youth centre's work in educational terms.

Youth centres are usually seen by the public at large as a means of containment or social control; it 'keeps them off the streets'. Youth workers loathe this phrase – it devalues what they are doing. But, to be fair, they are not entirely without blame for this popular misconception. They have been less than clear about what they mean when they talk about the educational value of youth work. Practitioners frequently discuss their aims in such all-embracing, grandiose terms that it is possible to justify almost any activity within their scope. This is the kind of self-delusion which does not inspire confidence.

Having said this, it has to be recognized that even if the work of the youth centre could be demonstrated to have educational value in terms of social development, this still would not satisfy my friend. She would, indeed, have seen this as cause for further unease. Not only was the primary task of the church not being tackled but scarce resources were being drawn into a secondary one. For Christians committed to informal education this is the crux of the problem. They find themselves under threat from two directions. On the one hand they suffer with their secular colleagues from the misconceptions of the public at large. On the other hand they come under attack from other Christians who see them as avoiding and even detracting from the churches' primary task. It is this double-edged pressure which has led to the withering away of much Christian informal education. Secular youth workers find it difficult enough to justify their approach in terms of measurable effect. It has to be admitted that Christian informal education has apparently been singularly ineffective in carrying out the churches' primary task.

The model of the Christian educator has long been that of the up-front preacher/evangelist who lays it on the line. Right across the board in the modern Christian community it is assumed that education means formal education. Anything else is viewed with misgiving and frequently rejected by 'the person in the pew' as a waste of scarce resources – to the chagrin of those within the church whose vision of education is wider. Christian formal education has moved on from the days of 'chalk and talk'. It is often imaginative, makes use of the latest educational approaches and can be extremely effective in producing a well-informed committed Christian community. This very sophistication further threatens the informal, particularly at a time when resources – finance and personnel – are becoming increasingly scarce. There was a great blossoming of informal education in the form of Christian youth clubs in the 1960s. This is fast withering away. Most Christian youth centres are born and die in an atmosphere of hostility and suspicion. They survive in spite of, rather than because of, the local Christian community.

Secular colleagues need to take warning. In the present climate they too could find themselves under threat from more thought-out educational approaches. Unless we are all prepared to produce a well-argued justification for informal education we will not survive. Above all, this justification needs to point to measurable results. All-embracing vagueness will simply no longer do. If this is difficult for the secular educator, it is infinitely more complex for Christians. For not only must Christian workers have clear educational aims to meet the requirements of a secular society where resources are dwindling but they must also be able to demonstrate that informal education is an appropriate vehicle for communicating the Christian message. If the first task is difficult the second appears to be beyond the reach of our present thinking.

Oddly enough the starting point for this revolution lies in the work of Jesus himself as portrayed in the gospels. It could be argued that he was an early practitioner of informal education. There is a danger in this sort of approach. The life of Jesus is so potent and pregnant with meaning that groups as diverse as Marxists and right-wing fundamentalists have been happy to claim him for themselves. Having said this the fact remains that Jesus used the principles now enshrined in informal education to great effect. He gathered around him a large informal group of men and women ranging from the famous twelve Apostles to a wide variety of more or less interested 'followers'. He drew these people into a shared experience that challenged their values. His teaching was largely informal – like his fascinating use of parable. These apparently simple folk tales have defied analysis in academic terms. In them Jesus threw the responsibility for learning back into the control of his hearers: 'Those who have ears to hear let them hear'. Even his more formal teaching had an enigmatic quality which has bewildered those seeking formal concepts and thought-out philosophies. Again, the effect of this is to leave control in the hands of the hearers, who are challenged to rethink their values systems and to begin to develop a radical alternative life style. Hardly any of Jesus's teaching was devoted to organization; the whole movement was left flexible and informal – still a cause of anguish within the church. This had a startling and dramatic consequence which was apparently quite intentional. The marginalized people or society were drawn right into the heart of the movement. Conversely the experts, those whose formal education gave them access to institutions of religion and state, found themselves pushed to the fringe, unable to understand.

Here we confront the central issue which the challenge of informal education sets before the Christian community. Those who find themselves denied access to power in society develop for themselves a whole informal framework in which they operate with great skill and effectiveness. They value little the much vaunted fruits of formal education because they understand instinctively that the whole system is designed to deny them access to the power structures. It is this aspect of informal education which has received scant attention. The method you use to educate determines the client group with which you work. The further you move into the realms of formal education the more 'up market' your client group becomes. This is inevitable and inescapable. Therefore your choice of method in education actually reveals your value system. It reveals who you believe to be a priority group. I have heard Christian workers boast of the way in which their youth work became more effective in terms of the churches' primary task when they shut down their youth club and moved to a more formal approach. 'We were just wasting our time – now we see results for our labours.' This sounds all very fine until it is undertood that they not only shut the youth club, but also excluded from their work most of the members. Their work became 'more effective' because they moved to working with a client group who could appreciate a formal educational approach.

The much maligned youth club is still the only effective method yet devised to reach the marginalized young people of our society. Every step taken down the road that leads from informal to formal leaves behind increasing numbers of these young people. That is why all the sophisticated talk in youth work today which leads away from basic grass roots informal education must be resisted. The Youth Service, for all its faults, is all some of these youngsters have. It is the only setting in which they can learn in a way which is appropriate to them.

In the Christian context we are further constrained because we claim to be disciples of Jesus. I have already suggested that his use of the informal drew into the centre of his work the marginalized, powerless groups of his day. This was, I believe, no accident but a clearly thought out, premeditated strategy, an integral part of his teaching about the Kingdom of God. At the very heart of his message lay this concept of the kingdom or rule of God. He taught that one day this kingdom would supersede all other rule and all other authority. For now it was anticipated in his work and was to be anticipated in the life of his followers. They were to live out God's tomorrow – today! The kingdom Jesus described has been aptly described as the 'upside-down kingdom'. In the kingdom of God the accepted value systems of this present age are turned on their head. What is highly valued in one is nonsense in the other. The people considered most important in one are considered to be of the least importance in the other. In his ministry Jesus demonstrated what it would be like when God was in charge. He deliberately chose methods of communication which empowered and gave value to those who were considered outcasts. In the closing hours of his life he was to come face to face with those who 'really mattered'. To their utter amazement he was to remain almost totally silent in their presence. That silence was the most eloquent indictment of their whole value system.

It follows from this that those who today claim to be his followers need to live out the principles of the 'upside-down' kingdom. They need to prioritize time, effort and resources for those whom this society sends to the back of the queue. And because informal education appears to be the best tool we have yet devised to accomplish this, our commitment to it must not be allowed to falter.

Having said all this we must not delude ourselves. Those who advocate the use of informal educaton in the Christian context must be honest enough to admit that it appears to have been largely ineffective in terms of the churches' primary task. Again, this problem is paralleled in the secular field. Secular informal educators have the greatest difficulty in describing, in terms that can actually be measured, what it is they are achieving in such a way as to convince their critics. We all take refuge at this point in vagueness. We are achieving a lot – the problem is just to quantify it. We may point to the progress some person has made towards self-fulfilment, but who is to say that that progress would not have been made anyway with time? Inexorably, we feel ourselves, in youth work terms, being pushed into the 'keep them off the streets' syndrome. Christian youth workers are even more at risk. Where the advocates of formal Christian education can point to positive results in terms of Christian young people – committed, informed and aware, we can only point to an occasional flicker of light here and there quickly extinguished by the cold water of peer pressure. And so we have got a problem and we need to admit that. I do not believe there is one Christian youth worker who has not wondered whether all this informal education is not a waste of time and effort. Many have given up under the pressure of external hostility and internal doubts. Those who have survived have done so only because they are convinced that this approach is the only one capable of serving the young people with whom they are in contact. They know that to give up their commitment to informal education is to relinquish their commitment to the most needy young people in society. They are not prepared to do this and therefore they hang on with a sort of grim determination, hoping against hope for some kind of breakthrough.

In broad terms this is the present state of the art in Christian informal education: the determination of a dwindling band of youth workers to keep faith with a commitment. However, to remain in this ideological no man's land would be to invite disaster. Eventually Christian informal education would just be a thing of the past, swamped by a confident and successful formal approach which was blind to its élitist tendencies. It is essential that we press forward in our thinking, that we ask hard questions about the apparent failure of the informal approach in terms of the churches' primary task: that we formulate new initiatives for the future.

We have been speaking of formal and informal education as separate entities. Of course they are not; they are rather a continuum shading gradually into one another. Standing at either *A* or *B* and viewing the other side can be enlightening. The teacher standing at point *B*, committed to highly structured formal compulsory education, is aware that this approach is inappropriate, and in some cases, positively damaging to pupils, particularly those who are 'least able' in academic terms. The formal approach denies them a sense of personal worth and continually reinforces a negative self-image by persistently presenting them with evidence of their inability to cope. Many teachers are aware that the skills and attitudes developed in informal education are ideally suited to these young people. Many have initiated experiments in informal approaches. Whether these initiatives can survive in the present educational climate is a matter of conjecture.

On the other hand the informal educators who find themselves at point *A* are aware of the strengths of the formal approach. They find

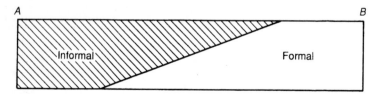

Figure 7.1 Formal and informal education.

their efforts continually misunderstood and what little progress they make swept away by the combined forces of peer pressure and cultural norms. They have an urge to say loud and clear 'that is not what I meant . . .' They long to be able to motivate and mould attitudes in the way they perceive possible in the formal field.

In Christian informal education this urge to say something has often found overt expression in what is generally termed 'the epilogue'. At some point in the programme, usually towards the end of the evening, members are gathered together and given a talk about some aspect of the Christian faith. To the secular youth worker this appears very strange – a total turn around in the whole ethos of the proceedings. However odd it may seem it is an attempt to overcome the basic weakness inherent in informal education: that it is continually prey to misunderstanding. Informal education is rather like watching a film without the soundtrack. Viewers are left making up their own minds as to what the story might be about. The simpler the plot the easier this task becomes. *Shoot out at the OK Corral* would be fairly self-explanatory with or without its soundtrack. But the more complex and subtle the plot the more difficult the task of interpretation becomes. A film based, for example, on a Jane Austen novel would be almost unintelligible without its soundtrack. So it is with informal education – it communicates high-profile, accessible concepts well. But when the message becomes more complex, communication is inclined to break down.

It is important to understand why this is so. Viewers base their interpretation of what they see on their already formulated world-view. The more the plot is at odds with that worldview, the more misunderstanding is likely to result. Viewers filter what they see through their own perspective on life; the message is annexed to their own worldview and its power to challenge and transform attitudes is severely weakened. This is why Christian informal education has been apparently ineffective in terms of the churches' primary task. Workers have been trying to communicate a worldview which challenges that of their clients at almost every point. The young people have only their own worldview to help them interpret what is happening. Take an example. A young man breaks into the club and causes damage or steals. Despite this he is readmitted to the centre. The Christian staff team believe that this will communicate the concept of forgiveness. But nothing of the sort is communicated. The young person reinterprets the action in terms of his own worldview. According to this, he has simply been lucky enough to come across a bunch of suckers.

There is no way that attitudes can be changed on this basis. The young person would find it difficult to survive with this Christian attitude within his own culture. It appears to be possible only in the sheltered, unreal world apparently inhabited by the staff of the centre. The film devoid of its soundtrack has failed to communicate its message. The Christian concept of forgiveness is a complex one. Our forgiveness of others is based on God's forgiveness for us. This was made possible by the death of Jesus on the cross. Jesus took the decisions which led to his death 'on the street'. It was a course of action that was deliberate and challenged every accepted attitude to power and status now and then. This radical message is watered down to the inexplicable behaviour of a gang of well meaning suckers!

It is because informal education is continually swallowed up by cultural norms that we find ourselves with so little to show for our endeavours. This is particularly true of the Christian informal educator. The work is both complex and radical – but this is also true for the secular informal educator. Our centres become fantasy worlds divorced from the harsh realities of life outside. We had hoped that they would be centres of learning and renewal. Clients pass through untouched – with most of their attitudes intact. The solution is obvious: the film needs a soundtrack. The question is, how is the soundtrack to be supplied? The answer in Christian youth clubs has been to provide an 'epilogue'. But this is to insert a chunk of formal education into the informal. The club night runs its course and then we suddenly change gear. However imaginatively this is done eyes become glazed as minds go into neutral. Young people frequently interpret what is happening in the light of their only other similar experience – the RE lesson at school. When the response to the epilogue is less than encouraging it is concluded that these young people have 'no interest in Christian things'. Soon the pressure is on to move away from the informal, i.e. close the club.

The difficulty all this exposes is simply expressed. We have been so inclined to see the formal and informal as separate entities that if we move away from one we rapidly find ourselves drawn into the other. We are caught between two magnets: if we break free from the field of one we find ourselves stuck on the other. But this insistence on either/or is our problem. There is another possibility of learning to operate in the area where the formal and informal shade into one another. This is the area indicated by *XY* in Figure 7.2.

I am convinced that this subtle blend of the formal and the informal is the solution to our difficulties. But here we are on the

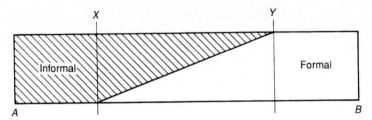

Figure 7.2   Formal and informal education – the arena for intervention.

edge of largely unexplored territory. We are seeking to communicate the Christian message to some of the more alienated people in our society. Informal education is continually absorbed into their already formal perspectives, which are the fruit of much bitter experience. Formal education is just a complete turn off and can survive only when backed either by compulsion or some sort of bribe – 'you can only come to club if you stay for and behave in the epilogue'. But if we could blend together the formal and informal so that they belonged together as naturally as film and soundtrack . . .

How might this be achieved? To the best of my knowledge this is largely unknown terrain in both the secular and Christian fields. We have all made expeditions into it. Sometimes they have been planned, though more often than not it has been a chance experience in the midst of the ordinary that has filled us with a sense of what might be. We have been unable to sustain the position. Old ideas have hauled us back into their secure grip. Pressure of time and fear of failure have added their deadly discouragement.

At this point I frequently find myself meditating on a story from the Old Testament. After much wandering the people of Israel had arrived in the wilderness at the very borders of the promised land. They sent spies to check things out. These men returned with glowing reports of a land flowing with milk and honey. However they also brought tales of insurmountable difficulties – walled cities and, would you believe – giants. Discouraged by these tales of woe the people turned back into the wilderness and a whole generation were to perish before they again stood on the borders of the good land. If we continue to draw back it could be equally disastrous for us. There are certainly plenty of prophets of doom who urge retreat with tales of the problems that lie ahead. But it is vital that we press on to explore this crucial area where formal and informal merge (*XY*).

But is this all that can be said – just a rousing call to arms? I do not believe so. The other point of that Old Testament story is that the spies brought back actual evidence of what lay ahead. We are told that they carried back a bunch of grapes so large that it had to be carried on a pole between two bearers. We too have brought back fruits from our promised land, which could be evidence of good things to come. I should like to draw attention to three of these.

The first is participation. I almost hesitate to mention this. I can, indeed, hear the groans and yawns with which its mere mention will be greeted – the concept has become such a bandwagon. It appears to be seen as some kind of cure for all ills in areas such as the Youth Service, adult education and community work. Having said this, there is no doubt that work in the area *XY* where the formal and informal shade into one another will be essentially participatory. Unless our life together is truly a shared experience there are no channels along which ideas can flow. We need to ignore the unease we feel at jumping on the latest bandwagon. I am not talking about members and consultative committees and the like. These methods, with all their pseudo-political and pretentious paraphernalia are really firmly rooted in the formal élitist area of education. They create a false impression of participation but can be continually manipulated by those skilled in their operation. I am rather suggesting exploring non-élitist informal channels for discussion and decision making. These need to take on the cultural ethos of those participating in them. This starting point means asking how individuals go about making decisions and then going on to ask how these processes can be built into our work.

Secondly, I would suggest that the message we wish to convey needs to be explicit in the informal and formal alike. Otherwise the formal soundtrack will be out of synchronization with the informal experience. This may mean making some very hard decisions about our programmes. We need to identify what it is we wish to communicate and then look for those activities and experiences that put the message across. It is when this blend of medium and message have fortuitously come together that we have glimpsed the promised land. There is another aspect to all this. It is impossible to communicate a radical message to others unless you are prepared to live it out yourself. Christian informal educators are part of their own message. There is a little Christian jingle that goes, 'What you are speaks so loud that the world cannot hear what you say'. If our faith is some kind of part time hobby, like golf or stamp collecting, it will certainly have little impact on those who have already formed their perspective on life through much hard-won experience.

Thirdly, there is a whole range of activities that have within their very structure this blend of formal and informal. These need to be given a much higher profile within our work. Drama, art, music, simulation games – done unpretentiously – could all help us further along the road we wish to travel. These methods all engage the interest and attention of participants – the great strength of informal education. However, at the same time, the educator remains in control of the message being relayed – the strength of formal education. They therefore offer exactly the sort of subtle blend of formal and informal that we are seeking. We may feel inexperienced in these areas but this can facilitate learning together.

This, then, seems to me to be the present position in Christian informal education. To fail to recognize the weaknesses inherent in the approach would be to court disaster and would ultimately lead to a complete abandonment of informal education within the Christian community, at least, by those who saw the churches' primary task as an educational one. But to abandon the informal in this way would be at the same time to abandon those people for whom the formal is totally inappropriate. To find the subtle blend of formal and informal suggested above is a difficult undertaking. It must now become our aim to work this out in practice.

It is worth remembering that though this territory is new and strange for us, it has not always been so within our own culture, nor is it so in many Christian communities worldwide. There is stored away in the Christian community a vast resource of experience in cross-cultural communication. This reaches back, as we have seen, to the methods used by Jesus himself. John begins one of his letters with these words:

> We write to you about the Word of life which has existed from the very beginning. We have heard it, and we have seen it with our eyes; yes we have seen it and our hands have touched it.

This 'hands-on' experience of the Christian faith is what we must be determined to provide within our work, for nothing less will suffice for the people to whom we are committed.

CHAPTER 8

Working with carers

PAULINE GERTIG

Community care policies have encouraged people suffering from dementia to be supported in the community rather than institutions. This has highlighted the important role played by carers and the pressures placed upon them. With the marked rise in the numbers of people aged 80 between now and the end of the century the need for additional professional support for carers has become more widely acknowledged. Yet as the Department of Health and Social Security (DHSS) stressed to the local authority sector, their expected role will be to 'sustain and where necessary to develop but never to displace such support and care' (DHSS 1981: paras 1–9). This policy has been translated into practice by local authority Social Services Departments (SSD) in a number of ways.

The provision of formal services such as home helps, specialist day and respite staff can play a substantive role in preventing the build up of stress in carers (Levin, Sinclair and Garbach 1983). Such resources are often inadequate, over-stretched, geographically inconvenient and too inflexible to provide the ideal type of support a carer needs. However, where available and flexible they can and often do provide positive support. Community care policies have generally led to the enhanced deployment of a variety of staff with a remit to provide support for carers. Within this category can be included home helps, residential staff and field social workers. It is the service provided by this latter group which is to be the central focus of the chapter.

Field social workers operate from many varied settings and, given the pattern of employment policies within these, are often able to adapt and reformulate the style and content of the service they deliver. It is therefore not without risk to make generalizations. There is a wide variety of intervention which can be offered by field social workers, including individual casework, family therapy, group and community work. For the purposes of this chapter I will concentrate on individual casework and group work and the potential they offer for informal education. In group work this tends to take the form of relative-support programmes, where carers can meet to discuss their common difficulties and offer one another support. Within this chapter I will be attempting to establish whether these two modes of intervention encompass elements of informal education and what advantages and or problems this brings when informal education is not the primary means of intervention.

Behind the rhetoric

The publication of a number of horrific accounts of institutional care (Townsend 1962; Robb 1967) neatly coincided with a general thrust in government policy towards the notion of 'community care'. It became popular among professionals as a perceived alternative to dehumanizing institutional care and with government ministers as a potentially cheaper option (for a discussion of the policy issues and debates surrounding the expansion of community care see K. Jones 1989). What needs to be stressed was the almost universal belief that, however ill defined the term, community care and care in the community for elderly people was preferable to that offered in institutions. Yet beneath the rhetoric lurked the reality that community care was largely care by families and overwhelmingly by women (Ungerson 1987), care which was to be undertaken with scant improvement in community-based services to help them to undertake the task. It is a situation highlighted within the Griffiths Report (DHSS 1988: para 9).

> Community care has been talked of for thirty years and in few areas can the gap between political rhetoric and policy on the one hand or between policy and reality in the field on the other hand been so great.

This report proceeds to recommend the creation of a minister and department with clear responsibility for community care to ensure that domiciliary and institutional care for the elderly and their carers are organized in a coordinated manner under the auspices of the local authority, with a structure that ensures the establishment of a single agency within a locality, which will be responsible for adequate service provision and which the carer can approach for services.

The operational structure of most SSDs, with respect to field social workers, operates via a referral procedure and individually held caseloads. This has meant that the contact of the majority of carers with this agency is pre-eminently through casework. Ideally this can offer carers a one-to-one supportive relationship in which they are able to explore the nature of the illness of the persons cared for; their response to caring; and the services that are available to enable the carers to cope with a profoundly difficult problem. It is a service which can be highly individual and tailored to carers' needs and which offers them direct access to professional advice and support. However, the lack of a statutory basis for involvement with this client group, coupled with the increase in the volume of work and staff reduction within SSDs in recent years, has meant that such a casework service is not always available. Group work, by providing mutual support for carers through the exchange of ideas and the development of networks, has been used to great advantage in this area of work. It would be wrong to see the two modes as simply alternative. They are best seen as complementary, part of a con-tinuum of support, able to operate both independently and in tandem to give the carer the support necessary to deal with the demands of the task.

We are currently experiencing a rise in the number of older people aged over 80 at a time when the overall numbers are beginning to fall. This shift in the balance of the elderly population is significant because it is among the older age group that the highest incidence of dementia occurs. Research has indicated that as many as 22 per cent of those over 80 suffer from dementia (Kay *et al* 1964). Dementia, which includes Alzheimer's Disease, progressively destroys the cells of the brain (Gray and Isaacs 1979). This leads to problems with self-care, memory and decision making. As the disease progresses these tasks may be increasingly assumed by spouses, children, friends and neighbours – people generally referred to as 'informal carers'.

Webb (1987) highlighted the extent to which carers (not exclus-ively those caring for someone with dementia) are isolated and highly vulnerable members of the community in terms of their own health, career prospects and income. Personal accounts from carers (Gilleard 1984; Mace and Robins 1981; Wright 1986) all graphically illustrate the debilitating effects of the tasks they undertake. Both the research and the accounts portray the frustration, isolation, guilt and anger experienced by so many, as well as the negative effect their role has upon their own health, privacy and life chances. Many carers wish to continue with their task but with some recognition and financial remuneration for their contribution. Addressing these issues requires a change of political will and is not the direct concern of this chapter. What is important is the extent to which it is possible to improve access to existing provision among carers and to provide the best possible levels of support for them within the current climate.

Can informal education, through the media of casework and work with relatives' support groups, play a role in enabling carers to perform their task? Initially both interventions are viewed as establishing a relationship between worker and carer, and carer and carer, in which the primary focus is support. By support in this context I mean the process by which social workers enable carers to unravel the complex emotional and practical issues their situation involves. This support can take a variety of forms: one-to-one counselling; information and advice giving on such matters as benefit entitlement; arranging the provision of practical services; and offering the carer the opportunity to learn about the nature of dementia and its effects on the sufferer and the carer. If we look at each in turn, we can see elements which are present in the process of informal education (Smith 1988: 134–49). The important point to stress here is that the boundaries of the work and intervention clearly intrude, at all levels, into an educational arena, transcending that of the mere provision of a supportive service.

Casework and informal education

On the basis of the discussion of informal educational methods already mentioned, and in the introduction to this book, it can be seen that casework, as normally understood by social workers, offers opportunities for such interventions. Casework and, more specifically, the elements of practice that might be considered as educational, takes place in a variety of settings: the carer's home, the hospital unit, if the person with dementia attends for assessment or a residential home, if the person with dementia attends for day care or regular respite care. In all these settings the carer is exposed to different professionals, medical and nursing staff, residential and social workers all of whom can offer information, advice, education and generalized training in the care of those suffering from dementia and in recognizing personal needs. Each professional in an individualized way, for example, the workers in a residential home, provide a vital link for carers in sharing the task of caring. They are able to discuss the management of behaviour and through this interaction the residential workers can come to perform an educative role even though this may not be perceived as being their primary function.

Education implies that the process of learning is deliberate and purposeful and that the people concerned are seeking to acquire knowledge (see Chapter 1). In the casework relationship this is not always the case. Carers may prefer not to know or may even ignore the existence or scale of a given problem in the hope that it will go away. This highlights a conflict in orientation between the educator and the caseworker. The informal educator assumes that the learner wishes to attain knowledge or some skill or attitude. That is to say they possess some autonomy or choice about the matter and positively elect to learn. The object of the learning may not be clearly recognized by any of the parties. It is unlikely to take the form of a neat package of learning objectives. It will rather consist of a generalized wish to 'know more' about an identified area. The caseworker may be in a position of having to persuade the carer to accept particular training or to acquire certain knowledge, some of which may be unpleasant, uncomfortable or challenging. From the perspective of the caseworker this is undertaken in the interests of the carer's well-being as well as that of the person with dementia. Participation in the process of learning may not therefore always be voluntary and this can entail difficulties for the caseworker. How far should someone be persuaded to learn and acquire knowledge that they do not want? The process of getting the carer to acknowledge the need for learning may be the initial focus of intervention. Indeed it may be the only role performed by the caseworker as the subsequent educational experience can take place outside the boundaries of this relationship. The transmitting of information and the enabling of learning may not be achieved in the short term.

All this is not without inherent risks and certainly does not have to be undertaken by the field social worker. Indeed some people may find that other professionals such as doctors or community psychiatric nurses are a more helpful and appropriate source of information. The process of giving information in the casework relationship may intensify the carer's sense of resentment towards the person with dementia. For not only do they have to cope with the mechanics of caring but they are also 'expected to understand all this new information'. This learning can also create a watershed in the relationships between all parties when the knowledge spells out the real extent of dependency. In saying this we should not lose sight of the fact that similar problems and tensions can arise in the work of informal

educators in other settings. They do not enter professional relationships on a value-free basis. However, many do not have statutory responsibilities of the social worker and are hence potentially
freer when making interventions to focus on the client.

In individual casework – where time constraints allow – the
timescale of learning can vary depending on the needs of the carer.
Some carers may opt to engage in an immediate and intense learning
experience. Others chose to develop their learning according to the
demands of their situation. As a result the timescale and pattern of
learning can be idiosyncratic. Given this and other factors, the
learning must inevitably take a variety of forms. Within this setting
flexibility is not an optional extra but an essential precursor for
success.

The individual casework relationship is an ideal medium for
addressing the cultural expectations placed on carers as well as their
wider social system, network and cultural norms. Interventions and
content must to a degree, therefore, be tailored to match consumer
expectations – something which is additionally difficult in more
formal educational channels. Often those who are most likely to be
carers, that is to say women (Lewis and Meredith 1988), are those for
whom it is most difficult to utilize the more formal channels of
education because of the very demands placed on them by their
tasks. Attendance at an evening class is possible only if you have the
money to pay, the time to go, adequate transport, public or private
and access to a competent sitter. Cultural expectations can often
prohibit women from using these channels unless these and other
deeper issues linked to gender oppression are addressed. Intervention via the casework relationship, it must be stressed, can be adapted
to the carer's social system and network. If the carer is isolated then
discussion can focus on how this isolation can be reduced and
alleviated, on how to get help from sources untapped or under-
utilized such as churches and neighbours.

Limitations of the casework approach

There are a number of limitations to the purely casework approach in
work with carers. It can be expensive of worker's time. It relies
heavily on the knowledge and competence of an individual social
worker. Given the rise in specialist workers in SSDs, there are now a
growing number who have a sufficiently extended degree of competence, interest and concern for carers to undertake this form of
intervention. However, this is not always guaranteed and carers may

receive a less than adequate service if they are totally reliant on social workers for learning opportunities. The casework relationship also reinforces their isolation for it is unlikely to introduce them, as a matter of course, to other carers. Some social workers and managers may wish to keep carers isolated: individual clients are much less prone to challenge service providers. Isolation can therefore function as a useful mechanism for rationing resources. Such limitations are familiar to practitioners and have often been the impetus under-pinning other methods of intervention such as relatives' support groups. However, there are a number of difficulties in establishing group work practice especially in what is essentially an individual casework agency dominated by an orientation towards the individual.

Group work in SSDs is often perceived as something 'extra' undertaken by social workers in addition to their existing casework. Where group work is seen as valuable, it may be taken into account as part of a social worker's workload. However, this is not always the norm and this type of intervention has become increasingly threatened by reductions in resources through ratecapping. In most SSDs this has encouraged a concentration on statutory work, es-pecially given the publication of a number of 'critical' reports and legal inquiries on their handling of child care issues.

Where social workers have sought to establish relatives' support groups they often encounter resource difficulties such as the lack of suitable premises, funding and the time to effectively organize the groups. In view of these difficulties it is to the credit of many workers that so many relatives' support groups have been estab-lished and continue to operate successfully. Not surprisingly in cases where the same worker undertakes both roles – combining a case-work with a group work service – conflict may occur.

The problems of undertaking both roles are clear. The carer may feel unable to criticize the service given by the social worker in light of new learning undertaken in the group setting. The level and type of learning gained within the group may be a repetition of what has already been achieved within the casework relationship. The carer may feel uneasy about revealing negative attitudes towards the sufferer in front of the worker. Yet there are advantages in undertak-ing both roles. One is that the social worker and carer are partners within the group and can share a mutual learning experience which may alter the parameters of the power relationships between them. An exchange of ideas between them can potentially restructure their relationship to the benefit of both. Where social workers undertake responsibility for the running of the group they are more likely to be sensitive to the particular problems faced by the carer. They may consequently be able to influence the curriculum of the group to ensure that it addresses particular learning needs. The process of informal education can be continued into the group setting in a way which is compatible and consistent. It can further be argued that this consistency is crucial as it offers carers an identifiable person who is aware of their particular problems, to relate to. However, whether the work is undertaken by the same person or not is often a question of resources, interest and commitment rather than choice.

Relatives' support groups as a medium for informal education

The relatives' support groups we discuss here are for those who care for people with dementia. Such groups are well established through-out the country and are run by a variety of practitioners, social workers, nurses and occupational therapists. The groups seek to encourage mutual support for carers and provide a forum for discussion on causation, treatment and management of dementia. In what way do these groups comply with the model of informal education?

Attendance is voluntary: carers opt to join although they are often initially unclear as to what they will get from the group. Meeting other carers facing the same difficulties as themselves and having the opportunity to share similar problems are often the main incentives. The group can be held in a variety of settings – a community centre, the lounge of a sheltered housing scheme or a room in a hospital. None of these venues has an overt educational function. The group can also be community based and bring together carers living in a particular neighbourhood. Alternatively, it can develop as a con-sequence of an attachment to a particular organization such as a day unit or residential home. As far as timescale are concerned a survey of literature (Rawlings and Peacock 1986; Lodge and McReynolds 1983; Linge 1986) on the development and organization of relatives' groups indicates two general models: a short-term group which will meet over a period of 8–10 weeks for up to 1.5 hours per week and a long-term group which tends to operate on a monthly basis. Both aim to provide support and education for carers.

Short-term groups often have a structured programme of topics, speakers and discussions to be addressed within a given time span. The content of the programme can be designed to take account of the particular problems faced by individual carers and will often include inputs from various specialists such as psychogeriatricians, community psychiatric nurses, psychologists and welfare rights officers. The course content need not be fixed and is often tailored to address the particular needs of the carer. If one carer is facing a problem with incontinence then this topic can be covered. Such flexibility enables particular problems to be addressed in a manner which would not be possible in a more formal setting. The curriculum can be structured to meet the expressed needs of the group. It can also be organized to take account of the particular life-style and social network of the carer and sufferer, e.g. a sitting service can be made available if the sufferer is unable to be left. This is often essential for the lack of such provision often prohibits carers from making use of more formal types of educational provision.

It is not only the provision of a sitting service which differentiates this type of education from that offered within more formal channels. The setting of the group in a lounge of a sheltered housing project or the day room in a hospital assessment unit, both with the availability of comfortable chairs and refreshments, helps to generate an informal atmosphere. People are not sitting behind desks, as they would be in a classroom environment. The emphasis is on informality and ensuring that participants feel comfortable enough to be able to discuss often highly personal and painful experiences. This would be difficult to achieve in formal and institutional settings. The style of leadership is equally important. Leaders play a key role in encouraging an informal but structured atmosphere – a balance which can be difficult to achieve. Professional leadership should not be assumed to be a permanent feature, for these groups are often a prelude to informal meetings organized by the carers themselves.

Such groups provide a forum which mixes support with education. They allow the carer legitimate time away from the sufferer while partially serving to fulfil their own social needs. Almost by definition it is difficult for carers to make full use of social and recreational facilities without the availability of adequate sitting services. Elements of self-help and support can therefore form an important aspect of such groups. By encouraging participants to talk freely about the difficulties of caring for someone with dementia they are able to offer mutual advice on particular problems. Through involvement in the group work process participants are simultaneously engaged in the process of learning for themselves while educating other carers. This support can and often does exceed the boundaries of the group, e.g. carers will contact each other between group sessions. It is certainly much rarer for the mutual support generated through the informal nature of the group to be an element within more formal educative processes.

The prime medium of exchange in the group tends to be dialogue: between carer and carer, between group leader and carer and between guest 'speaker' and carer. Dialogue in this setting not only offers participants the opportunity to expand their knowledge of themselves and the problems they are dealing with but also offers access in an informal setting to various professionals. Service organization has traditionally tended to militate against informal access to professionals. Involvement by them in this type of education makes them much more accessible to service consumers. Comments and criticisms of local authority and NHS provision are usually channelled through formal bodies such as councillors or community health councils. Meeting service providers in an informal setting not only provides an alternative opportunity for questions to be answered but also the chance for consumers to engage in a dialogue. The learning process is consequently not all one way. Comments, advice and complaints from carers in this setting all encourage professionals to both question and amend their practice.

An example of the two-way process inherent within this type of informal education has been the development of a carer referral system linked to an assessment service for people suffering from dementia. In seeking to improve their practice one local assessment unit organized a public meeting, to which both carers and professionals were invited, in order to sound out opinions on future service development. On the day, only professionals turned up. To redress this balance an additional meeting was arranged targeted solely at carers and a sitting service was provided. From this meeting, which attracted a substantial number of carers, it was established that what they wanted was a means whereby informal access to professionals, who had some knowledge of dementia, might be facilitated. As a direct consequence a 'drop in/self-referral' system was established which offered carers in the given locality such access to professionals. This service not only allowed a much greater degree of professional accessibility but for the first time such contact was not dependent upon a carer's ability to convince a service giver of immediate need. The process of mutual discussion and dialogue was a key factor in changing the style of service delivery to forms and content which the carers themselves felt was most appropriate to their needs.

Developments such as this highlight the ways in which the process of informal education can lead to change. It also illustrates how dialogue can blur the roles between professionals and carers. It has been notoriously difficult for service consumers to establish access to those forums which possess the capacity to initiate or influence policy and practice. The providers and planners of services are usually remote from the consumers. By tapping into the local network of carers, the unit in question was able to develop forms of service far closer to the expressed wishes of the carers. Informal education through relatives' support groups had a direct impact upon both the content, style and quality of service delivery – a pay off rarely achieved via the use of more structured formal education.

The role of the leader or worker as facilitator in this type of group is crucial to group cohesion and mutual support. Although the emphasis may be on informal learning, group leaders need to have a clear appreciation of the aim and purpose of the group. It is important that the group leader is in a position to direct the group when circumstances dictate – for example, if the individual problems of one carer dominate the group. The informality of such groups can give the false impression that they can run themselves without structure or organization. This may be the case but it cannot be taken for granted and the group leader must be prepared to undertake, as a minimum, responsibility for practical arrangements and be aware of the need to offer a sense of direction and guidance until the group is sufficiently well established to assume control over these areas.

Organization of time, programme and the curriculum of the group so that it can be responsive to the learning needs of the participants must initially reside with the group leader. In the short-term group these elements will tend to be tightly controlled in order to give the group sufficient structure to enable it to function. As the group becomes more established, responsibility for the curriculum can be assumed by the carers. Indeed, the very idea of there being a curriculum as such may disappear (see Chapter 1). This can happen much more readily in an established group. The focus of this type of group tends to be labelled 'support', with 'education' apparently playing a secondary role. In many respects, this can be seen as a clear signal that the group is moving towards a more informal mode of operation. There is a transition here which has to be managed and enabled. The danger is often that the educational needs are lost sight of in the process of change; in other words, the shift is not so much between support and education, as from formality to informality. The organizational structure of the long-term group may be similar to that of the short-term group but the timescale and curriculum content need to be much more flexible if it is to take account of the expressed learning needs of the carers.

Advantages of group work for carers

Participation in a relatives' support group creates the opportunity for establishing mutually supportive informal networks. These have enormous potential for helping to relieve and reduce isolation. They further offer the opportunity for carers to participate in a process of informal education which can be responsive to their learning needs. They can decide what area/topics to discuss and they can assume increasing responsibility for the curriculum as the group becomes more established. The flexible time structuring of the group can be responsive to the demands of individual carers; the structuring of learning is therefore entirely dependent on the needs of the participants. This ensures a high degree of responsiveness and mutual learning between group leaders and carers. Informal education through group work offers the carer the opportunity to participate in an educative process which is much more responsive to needs than the usual channels of education, which can very often be rigid about such issues as timing and attendance – a rigidity which the carer may find difficult. The flexibility of informal education through group work and the attention to practical matters such as a sitting service enable the carer to participate in a way which other educational practice prohibits.

Ideological difficulties for the social worker

Should social workers be involved in the process of education, even on an informal level? Social work training concentrates on developing specific methods of intervention, forms of service provision and the implementation of legal responsibilities. The role of social worker as educator is not overt; so is it legitimate for social workers to be involved in this type of work? As we have seen, social workers have skills and knowledge to offer which fit into the model of informal education. Through the culling of elements drawn from both casework and group work they have the capacity to offer a service to carers that enables each of them to participate in a learning situation tailored to their needs outside formal educational channels. Even though education may not be seen as the primary focus of social work or the central role of social workers both it, and they, can nevertheless play a key role as educational providers. This is not unproblematic for either the agency and worker, not least because the informal educational process will almost inevitably bring a number of conflicts to the surface. The demands and expectations of carers are likely to be raised. Hard-pressed departments are increasingly likely to find it beyond their capacity to satisfy such expectations in the short term. The primary responsibility of social workers is the implementation of statutory responsibilities and their role as educators must dovetail with this. Increasingly it is the implementation of these statutory responsibilities, especially in the field of child care, which threaten to curtail the opportunities for social workers to carry out work which is not a statutory responsibility. Yet if social work is to avoid becoming a fire brigade and solely reactive service, it is essential that informal education programmes are initiated and encouraged.

CHAPTER 9

Where practice enlightens theory and theory enriches practice

ELIZABETH AFUA SINCLAIR

In this piece I will explore what it is to be a student in an institution which is committed to informal education. What expectations were held of this mode of study? How did students marry theory to practice? How did they manage the freedom to direct their learning? In considering these experiences I will look at the informal networks created by students themselves, at how and why these came about and whether they were useful in acquiring the skills needed to create informal learning situations in their work with young people. Throughout I have made particular reference to African and Afro-Caribbean experiences because of the historical link between having a British education and settling in Britain.

It is my view that when the skills of informal learning – self-motivation, self-direction, the ability to assess and evaluate, participation in dialogue, the ability to manage time, freedom and change – have been acquired and practised, the student is better able to use them in other settings.

Historical influences

The tradition of African and Afro-Caribbean students coming to Britain certainly dates back to the sixteenth century. In more recent times the attraction to a formal hierarchical system of education has been its offer of an opportunity to hold prestigious and powerful positions in society. No matter whether that society was in Ghana or Barbados, a formal meritocratic system assisted in maintaining colonial rule by providing its administrators. This system closely followed Plato's treatise on education in that each individual would receive schooling to primary level; beyond that only those who were deemed to have the capacity to govern proceeded.

The rise of church or mission schools increased the demand for education, which followed Platonic and British traditions. Children would enter the system at the age of six where they remained until the age of twelve; those who did not attain the required standard year by year were not promoted to the next class. At twelve there was a further examination to enter middle school followed by the Common Entrance examination for transfer to secondary school. Throughout, competition was of great importance and examination success was rewarded with scholarships to study in Britain. Some of the attitudes promoted by this system were: that being educated was a privilege to be earned; that one had to be competitive to succeed; that those who reached the highest goals would be the leaders of society; and that those who had failed to do so would be led.

It is the transition from a formal meritocratic system to an informal cooperative system that is the kernel of this study. I recall my own experience when I began school in Britain. I remember feeling very privileged, as the oldest of five children, at being given the opportunity to be at an English school. However, the reality of my schooling in Ladbroke Grove did not match my expectations. I was not forced to work and I was promoted regardless of how well I did in my end of year tests.

John Dewey, who may be considered a pioneer in informal education, influenced British educators from the 1920s onwards. Dewey argued that traditional formal methods of learning were largely barren. He believed that it was everyday human interactions that provided learning situations, rather than the formal tradition of learning by rote and passing examinations. He proposed four reforms which he felt were essential for a sound educational system. These were to make school life more relevant to the home environment and neighbourhood; to ensure that subjects such as history and science had a positive significance to the student's life; that instruction in the three Rs was to be carried out with everyday experience as the background; and that individual needs and abilities should be given adequate attention.

For Africans and Afro-Caribbeans the purpose of introducing a British education system was contrary to the above. It was intended as an imposition of one culture on another and did little to make learning relevant to the participants. I believe it also engendered the notion of being given something that belonged to someone else. A comment that comes to mind is of a student's mother saying, 'you na wake op an go to the people them school?' This, of course, is true wherever learning fails to relate to life.

Expectations

We can compare a young African or Afro-Caribbean entering a liberal British school in the 1950s and a mature student embarking on a course of further education with a commitment to informal learning. There would, for example, be a shared feeling of being given a great opportunity, a second chance. The mature student would feel some pressure to succeed, perhaps feeling it was a last chance or, as some students say, not wanting to let the side down. Going back to the home community without successfully finishing the course was not to be contemplated. Anna Craven (1968) in her book *West Africans in London* includes several case studies where students could not return to their families or countries because they had not been successful in their chosen careers.

The parents of young people coming to Britain would have expected their children to gain some form of higher education without the burden of pass by merit or cost of schooling. In the same way, mature students were attracted to assessment which did not include a written examination which they felt would lessen their chances of passing.

The 'once in a life time' feeling would have been present not only for young people coming to Britain, but also for the mature student whose life chances would be greatly increased by attaining a professional qualification.

Young people who came from Africa and the Caribbean would have found the system of education in Britain during the 1950s and 1960s 'liberal' compared with the formal competitive system which they would have experienced before. Similarly, the previous experiences of mature students would predominately have been those of the secondary modern school. This would have been equally formal and teacher directed. Some students thought of the liberal approach as a soft option since their learning was not policed. Changing this attitude to learning is the most important factor. If informal learning is seen as an easy or soft option, which of course it is not, then it is difficult for students to be motivated.

It is true that most students who embark on youth and community and many other professional courses will not have experienced anything like the strict formal schooling of African and Afro-

Caribbean students. Their experience may have been a little more progressive but their expectations of being told what to learn by an all-knowing authority would have been thwarted by having to adjust to informal ways of learning, to being asked to take responsibility and authority for their own learning.

Choosing informal learning

Why, then, do students choose institutions committed to informal learning methods? As for students of other modes of study, the experience is rarely what had been expected. They have many reasons for embarking on a course of further education. The social rewards of more money and status are of importance as many students have been in part-time employment, unemployed or in work which offered little job satisfaction. In many instances the course offers a personal challenge either to establish independence or to prove to parents, teachers or friends the ability to cope with two or more years of study. Students are attracted to the practical emphasis of, for example, youth and community courses. This often links to the practical experience or part-time training which many students had before they joined a course. Even by making the decision to do a course students were often conforming to attitudes and the socialization of their families, schools and work. They wanted to achieve recognition as professionals and in order to do so they needed some form of training which would confer professional status and in turn would bring economic rewards. For some, their concern that young people should play an active part in society without conforming to a hierarchical social system provoked the decision to apply to institutions which were non-hierarchical in their approach. For yet others their choice was determined by geographical considerations and successful interviews.

A great deal of importance is normally placed on the practical element of youth and community courses. This gives credit to what Dewey termed 'practical intelligence'. Students begin the course knowing they have some skill or knowledge to share. As was said earlier, the absence of an examination may have played an important part in their choice of course. Many students may have had negative experiences of both school and examinations or be worried about their writing skills or lack of paper qualifications.

The process

So what are colleges which use informal methods of learning offering students? The response to this question will be largely couched with reference to training for youth and community work. Having said that it is important to stress that the preparation for this area of work is in many respects not dissimilar to that offered students engaged in professional training for, say, teaching, social work and health visiting. First and foremost such a course offers the opportunity to practise the skills needed for a chosen area of work. This practise takes the form of practical placements. Practical experience is also gained by the structure of sessions: small seminar groups provide students with the face-to-face group participation that is central to youth work. Being part of large lecture groups, year groups or tutorial groups provides an experience which can be analysed in terms of their own and others' behaviour with reference to theories of group dynamics. Induction into theory may take place in the lecture, seminar or via reading. The opportunity to participate in a dialogical process of learning is present in group setting and in a more focused way during supervision of placements and individual tutorials, where knowledge, skills and attitudes are evaluated through discussion. Finally, students are encouraged to determine and direct their own learning needs. They can do this by participating in the formulation of course content, as in Aberdeen College of Education (Scottish Education Department 1987) or being responsible for programming some part of the courses as at Goldsmith's College (DES 1988b) and YMCA National College (DES 1986). But more fundamentally than that, students use the vehicle of tutorial supervision and self-assessment to determine their individual programme of learning, while feeding back their experiences to other students and staff.

In examining the process from the students' point of view I have drawn largely from my experience and conversations with other students. Because participation in the process is voluntary it is essential that students become, if they are not already, highly motivated. The HMI report for Aberdeen (1987) noted that '. . . because they had been involved in negotiating both content and approach students were highly motivated'. This involvement at Goldsmith's begins with the selection procedure, which often leads to a feeling of unease on the part of applicants about being assessed by students. My initial feeling about this approach was that students would not be objective, perhaps looking

for personalities which would fit in with the existing student
group.

Once on the course students are faced with the concept of self-
direction. The majority of students will have been part of an
education system based upon the formal tradition, even where
practice was liberal. So it is little wonder that many view their role in
the learning process as the passive receiver of information. This
makes informal learning a new and difficult experience to come to
terms with. In the first instance it gives the student greater freedom.
Initially this is generally attractive, as students are able to set their
own pace and eschew competition with one another. Some are
excited about making choices and decisions about their learning;
among others it provokes feelings of being cheated: 'I thought they
would just tell me and I'd get on with it'. Being told what to do every
step of the way can be extremely comforting. To remain in a position
of relative powerlessness means that you do not have to take
responsibility for what goes on; power is given to some outside
authority which can be blamed at a later date.

Students very quickly realized that along with freedom came
responsibility. Most engaged in a tug-of-war in the first few months,
if not for the entire course. After all, the course was trying to change
attitudes which had been with them for 25 years or more. An
example of the tug-of-war between responsibility and powerlessness could be seen when students talked of lectures which 'didn't
offer much'. This might be interpreted as meaning that the onus
should be on the lecturer to provide the goods, whereas the onus was
on the student to analyse why the session was unproductive. It may
be that the student will decide to opt out; but the responsibility must
be theirs. There is no option to 'pass the buck' in self-directed
learning. Some students recalled being confused, wondering if they
had made the right decision and questioning their ability to take
charge of their learning. Others found it new and exciting to be able
to follow up areas of study not in the college curriculum.

As a student the most difficult thing to grapple with is that you are
not in competition with other students and that at the end of the
course you would not be assessed in a competitive way. One student
put it this way: 'sometimes you think that some people haven't
worked as hard as you but you still get the same certificate but it's all
to do with how far they have got for themselves'. Informal education
is about personal growth and development. As students gained the
ability to play a full part in their learning so they began to question
some of the administrative boundaries. Choice of placements and

supervisors came up several times; the contention was that if students could determine their learning needs they should be able to select a placement which afforded them the opportunity to meet those needs.

On the question of supervision, black students queried not having the choice of a black supervisor, feeling that this would have enabled them to open up about their work sooner in both the tutorial and supervision sessions. If colleges do not have black members of staff they maintain the illusion of an all-knowing white authority, which reflects a society where power resides within white-peopled institutions. A black tutor or supervisor not only provides a visible role model with whom the student can identify, but may contribute a wealth of experience and understanding of African and Afro-Caribbean culture to the course content. Students of social work and youth work are vociferous in demanding that the work of black academics and practitioners is a part of course content.

I believe that this lack of representation raises the question 'how will what I'm learning relate to black youth?' This argument regarding authority and identity also relates to the question of gender. Professional courses in social and youth work attract a high percentage of women, for some of whom it will be the first time they have attended to their own needs and identity as people. It is feasible that they may find themselves adopting a submissive role during tutorial or supervision because of previously socialized attitudes. All this opens up an area of investigation about whether it is necessary to have the personal experience of being black to facilitate African and Afro-Caribbean students in a tutorial or supervision setting. What is important here is to note that some students can feel that they are unable to make maximum use of the tutorial or supervision session because of the gender or race of the supervisor.

Tutorial and supervision are central to informal learning within professional training. They provide the means of evaluating work methods and linking practice to theory. For most students these unfamiliar experiences brought confusion and anxiety. One response was to find a more familiar experience with which to compare tutorials and supervision. These ranged from the confessional where students could confess 'bad' work practice, to the oral examination of 'the course so far'. It is interesting that tutors and supervisors were often seen as having all the answers, at least at the start of the relationship. Students recalled long silences, wanting to change tutors or supervisors or skipping sessions. However, practice tends to increase skill which in turn lessens fears and anxiety. One student poignantly described tutorials as 'having your brain picked at with knitting needles' and then 'having them pulled through your nose'.

Yet the tutorial is important because, for the first time, attention is focused intensely on practice. Tutorials gave me the opportunity to develop the skill of thinking aloud and of opening out about my work. The other side of the coin, as one student agreed, is a risk of becoming dependent on the supervisor and being worried that in a professional work situation you may not be able to cope alone. Supervisors and tutors with differing styles of work, were compared and if you 'enjoyed' a session others suspected you had not learnt much – a very Calvinistic attitude.

Practical placements are one area where students generally feel comfortable because, in the main they have had considerable experience of it. During placements students were learning to look objectively at work, questioning their approaches and preferences. Placements also served to throw light on areas of work which were not in the student's repertoire: work with girls, work without a club base and so on. In this way students were able to determine their strengths and weaknesses in practice. A great deal of time at placements seemed to have been spent in the negotiation or explanation of the student role. A common complaint seemed to be that the college provided insufficient information. One student recalled that the centre worker had contacted her tutor to check up on what she had been assigned to do. This was in fact a placement of the student's own choice; any conversation about her work programme should therefore have been with her. The difficulty with informal learning within an institution is that outside contacts may not always value the methods of work or appreciate the student's part in the learning process.

Full-time placements provided the student with an experience closely akin to post-college employment. Students spoke of gaining confidence, being clearer about the type of work they would do after college and convinced that they could take on a full-time commitment. This experience was a little different for students on courses where a link was maintained with the college throughout the placement, either by tutorials, or by full days session at college. This seemed to take away the feeling of being totally responsible for one's own learning. For one student the experience was far wider than the work brief as it was the first time away from home.

Lectures and essays fitted more easily into the students' expectation of learning. This raised the question of how students are motivated. At the beginning of courses there has to be some positive feedback, which may come from tutorials and self- and or peer assessment. In order to move forward there needs to be an achievable goal. The timing of assignments, essays, placements and assessments provided these goals. One student remembered that each new task seemed more difficult than the last, but with each she gained more confidence.

Much youth and community work takes place in small groups or with individuals. Seminars and tutorials offer a way of learning about these situations while participating in them. It becomes easier to write an essay on 'The purpose of a task in groups' if you have observed and 'lived it'. It becomes possible to link the practical placements to what is happening within year groups and sometimes to this or that theory. This can enhance learning, offering a feeling of living a fact as opposed to merely reading about it.

Informal networks

In many instances the informal learning networks created by students followed the course structure and came about as a result of students looking for ways of coping with the demands the course made on them. My observations here about informal networks, reflect my own experience. The cohesion of my year group was influenced quite directly by the loss, very early in the course, of a social facility. A coffee bar was replaced by sophisticated vending machines. This gave us an external authority to unite against. A student boycott created an alternative – the bringing of flasks and snacks. This evolved into a more structured fund-raising activity for about a year and aided the growth of the students' informal support networks.

The small-group learning within the course was reflected in friendship and interest groups. Apart from general encouragement these groups allowed for a range of topics and issues to be discussed. One HMI report notes that the student interest groups reflected concerns which had arisen from field-work placements, that they provided a forum for exchange of information and experience and that participants were being encouraged to uestion their attitudes and values. Sometimes groups met informally as a result of a seminar or lecture where students wanted to explore a subject or draw on the experience and knowledge of other students. It was often in small informal groups that difficult attitudes to race and gender could be faced; larger formal groups tended to provoke 'fight or flight' tensions.

More individual encouragement was gained by having one or two other students to maintain contact with. These were students who knew most about one's own strengths and frustrations. Some students made use of the extra-curricular supervision which they had as practitioners in their previous working situations.

Friendship groups often serve as 'cultural fixes'; any year group will be made up of students from a variety of cultural backgrounds. So, whether students had travelled many miles geographically or not there was the need to be with people who understood 'where you were coming from'. Students often found that their own develop-ment took them away from their previous lifestyle and therefore away from friends, and occasionally family. Those who had partners often noticed the profound effect changes in them had on their partners and family. In friendship groups they were able to discuss these changes with other people who were going through a similar experience.

For black students it was important to explore the degree to which their learning might be separating them culturally from their com-munities. This gave them an opportunity to relate what they were learning to their past experience of working with black young people; to talk through how they might intervene in the future, knowing they would be operating in an environment where the young people they worked with might feel powerless, after years of alienation, to affect change in their lives. As professionals they would also need to counter institutional racism in a way the white workers would not. Many voiced a need to be together with other African/Afro-Caribbean students who would appreciate the oppor-tunity to discuss these and other issues. This area has to be addressed when considering the question of the need for black workers to work with black communities and for women to work with girls and women. Such groups start by sharing a great deal of common ground.

Informal networks created by students themselves offer situations in which learning occurs outside the formal structure of the course. It engages students in dialogue, which is in the main evaluative, while providing encouragement and motivation when times are difficult. One student recalled how after several discussions and workshops on racism a friendship group gave her support to continue the course.

Informal learning requires the identification of appropriate learning experiences and the creation of situations which will enable meaning to be derived from those experiences. The process has to be formally planned, with definite aims and clarity about the means of achieving them.

CHAPTER 10

Educating informal educators

TONY JEFFS AND MARK SMITH

Within informal education there is a tendency for personality, individual skills and motivation to be emphasized and for other elements to be overlooked. The belief is often encountered that informal educators are born rather than made. Such development as is needed concerns the drawing out of what is there and the enhancement of certain skills. This cult of the natural and the emphasis on the charismatic are understandable but need to be questioned and contained. As the preceding chapters have demonstrated, the thinking and behaviour associated with informal education are, for the most part, learnt. Practice is developed through sustained and critical reflection upon intervention. This, in turn, contributes to the building and maintenance of a body of theory consistent with informed action and analysis of practice. What we label as 'natural' or 'intuitive' is frequently nothing of the sort; rather, it is the interaction, at a largely non-conscious level, of our critical faculties with the environments and behaviours we encounter. In this chapter we take the view that those faculties can be educated and, as a result, practice developed. More specifically, we focus on the process of making professional informal educators.

If this form of pedagogy is to be a key element of welfare practice it cannot be unduly dependent upon the supply of those who by background or birth resemble the chosen stereotype. Nor must it simply be equated with a superior form of 'Redcoating', whereby an educational dimension is grafted on to leisure provision (Foreman 1987). Within specific areas questions of personality, background and attitude may be crucial but they are rarely fixed. This flexibility arises either from an ability to develop performance or from the possibility that others' perceptions of workers can alter. Certainly the observation and accumulation of 'good practice' has limited application in this respect. It would be fruitless to extrapolate from these in order to construct a genotype of the ideal informal educator. This is not to argue in some vague liberal way that it is within the capacity of all to be competent informal educators, any more than it would be rational to suggest that all have the ability to work in residential homes or in care teams. What we are saying is that all those engaged in face-to-face welfare practice should possess the potential to undertake effective informal educational work. Whether that potential is currently being developed, or is effectively harnessed, is another matter.

At this stage we would like to address three questions. Why do so many welfare practitioners avoid or fail to exploit informal education? What is the nature of the dominant, training orientation within the process of preparing professional welfare practitioners, and how does this orientation impede the development of informal education, and, more generally, reflective practice? How might welfare practitioners be better prepared and educated so that they may use informal education?

Avoiding informal education

Traditional welfare structures, incremental growth and professional boundaries have combined to restrict the usage of informal education. Education has become associated with particular organizational forms and modes of intervention. These can be evoked by the mere mention of schools, classrooms, teaching and college. They are popularly, and often professionally, perceived as both the sites and modes of educational practice. Education is consequently viewed as an unnatural interloper when transposed to other areas of welfare – a diversion from the 'real' task in hand, an indulgence. For social workers to approach informal education requires them to transcend layers of accumulated occupational wisdom and practice; that they cease to behave like 'social workers'. Unfortunately it cannot be assumed that informal education is axiomatically acceptable to 'educationalists' either. Indeed, it no more comfortably resides with them than elsewhere. While the different elements of practice discussed in Chapter 1 may find some acceptability within, say, schools, taken together they can constitute a form of pedagogy which many teachers find strange or threatening. Where the term 'informal education' has been used on a sustained basis in primary education it has generally taken on a rather different set of meanings from those suggested here.

The very fabric of existing professionalized practice is impregnated with a disposition towards established forms and a range of taken-for-granted understandings. These contribute to the unique character and identity of the various professional areas. They cannot be wished away. Lacking a 'natural' base, informal education has to reach some form of accommodation with existing strands of practice. Advancement has been further impeded by the general lack of an adequate cross-professional literature. Practice has tended to develop within specialisms without reference to other arenas. The great strength of informal education – applicability to variable settings – is turned against it.

Resilience of professional boundaries alone cannot explain the resistance to informal education. Innate conservatism does play a part but that is a far too one-dimensional explanation. We have to recognize that the social and economic environment in which occupational groupings and their ideologies are formed reflects concerns and interests which run counter to much that informal education stands for. The focus upon learners taking responsibility for their own learning, and the associated emphasis upon process, are not phenomenon likely to recommend themselves to those currently in control of the central state and other leading institutions. Indeed, the liberal or critical disposition of those often associated with informal education, if not seen as a threat, is certainly viewed with some derision by apologists for the New Right. In a market economy it is product that is important, rather than the human process of production. The prevailing measure of activity, profitability, is a purely material element. It says nothing about the experiences of those whose labours generate it. Inevitably, given the dominance of such an ideology, approaches which value process and human well-being either have difficulties in being understood or are dismissed as having scant economic worth. In the end it is not simply informality which presents a problem but the very values at the heart of the educational enterprise itself.

While the emphasis upon product and upon minimal investment in order to generate gain may hinder critical thinking, the romantic imagination has been a further handicap. A large number of informal educators display a contempt for theory and glorify the natural and the spontaneous. The idea that the best practice somehow springs from within goes very deep. Theory about informal education is therefore inadequate, and the literature scarce. Practitioners have rarely been offered a coherent alternative to the dominant modes. Where thinking does emerge it often has a bureaucratic focus. An example here is the stress upon setting in many academic considerations of informal education rather than on the totality of the pedagogic enterprise (see, for example, Jarvis 1987). The cult of the natural and the concern with activity are particularly strong in those arenas where informal education can be said to have assumed some significance – youth work and community work. Thus not only has practice theory remained underdeveloped, other forms of intervention have been seen as attractive. In the case of community work, those with a stronger theoretical perspective tended to turn away from informal education in the 1970s towards more direct interventions in local struggles (Thomas 1983: 32). Others focused more closely on the development or extension of services into particular neighbourhoods, rather than on enabling learning.

Rejection by practitioners of this form of pedagogy is also often explained in terms of workload rather than theory. It is a form of intervention that is attractive; but time and pressure allow scant space for it to be developed. This is difficult to counter. Workers may well have the rhythm and content of their day determined by management and presented crises. It is essential to differentiate between the extent to which this is a genuine explanation or merely a shroud to obscure a resistance to change. It must further be asked to what degree informal education might restructure working patterns in such a way as to overcome the pressures that seemingly restrict its applicability. Finally, it should be acknowledged that in many respects informal education and linked methodologies may not engender the smooth operation of bureaucracies and units. In the process of engaging in dialogue and education, previously passive clients and service recipients may become active in their demands of practitioners and agencies.

Informality may worry some practitioners, who perceive it as a threat to their status, sense of professional self and mode of working. These concerns may be familiar; they are certainly more confidently articulated. Less vocalized, but probably more widespread, is the unspoken fear on the part of many professionals that they lack the requisite knowledge and expertise to engage in the educational process. Inadequate levels of training, both initial and post-qualifying; an anti-intellectual ethos and an alarming absence of theory within almost all welfare settings, not least schools; structures and traditions which impede sustained reflection upon practice; and cultures which reward apparent activity and output, all combine to produce workforces which have difficulty in handling ideas and educational processes. Given that so many avoid engaging in educational activity, both formal and informal, themselves and perceive the reflective analysis of practice as threatening, it is hardly surprising that they recoil from generating such critical activity among those over whom they may exercise power. This percolates through the totality of welfare organization. It helps to shape the ways in which management manages and face-to-face workers interact with clients and contributes to an emphasis on skills training and the fetishization of management as the routes to service enhancement and individual advancement.

Training for failure

It is a truism that professional training courses, according to employers, validating bodies, academics and not least students, fail to address key issues adequately. Essential skills are not taught and topics skimped. Overload is the term often applied, both in the defence of training courses and as a justification for the rejection of additions to the curriculum. Introducing informal education into training courses, whether for social workers, teachers, youth workers, community health workers or priests, therefore requires substantive justification. Unless the parameters of the debate itself are restructured any case for the interjection of informal education into a given programme entails arguing for the removal of some existing areas of study.

Making space is not the problem, at least as presently debated. The problem, we believe, it is the prevailing orientation towards training (and skills) rather than education. The concern with profit and market inevitably entails an orientation towards product. Training, dedicated as it is to the inculcation of a limited range of competences, generally appears to be a more efficient route to creating an 'appropriate' workforce than does the more discursive and critical process of education. The concern with skill has been strengthened by the way in which policy makers, academics and practitioners have become beguiled by 'practice'. As Alexander (1988: 152) has argued in respect of primary school teaching:

> Despite the profession's ritualistic use of the words 'practice' and 'practical' in ways which suggest that teaching is little more than a simple manual activity, the job does in fact require a high degree of cognitive engagement.

The extent of the failure, deliberate or otherwise, to recognize the necessity of cognitive engagement obviously varies between institutions and professional groupings. A litmus test of the gravity of the problem is the extent to which talk of overload percolates any discussion about curriculum reform. One shortcut to such reform has been the energetic pursuit of minimalist training programmes. These seek to accredit practitioners and enhance their skills to meet a limited range of approved tasks. The methodology for achieving this is not fixed. It can entail the retrospective accreditation of experience, the adoption of low-level apprenticeship style training and part-time employer-led programmes. Programmes are often dressed in the progressive clothing of openness, access and flexibility. Yet underpinning many of them is a desire to limit critical thought and to undermine the autonomy of practitioners. The current situation in youth and community work is a good example of this (Jeffs and Smith 1987; 1989). The confused and confusing debate about social work training demonstrates another. Exchanges about the desirable length of training and essential competences often amounting to an unspoken conflict between parties seeking training at the expense of education and vice versa (C. Jones 1989).

Within the present climate, created by a government that sees itself as the herald of free enterprise, the gathering pace of commitment to skill enhancement and the measurement of product is hardly surprising. Yet when agencies operate from the basis that programmes can be more efficiently run if they ape Marks and Spencer's, they expose the superficiality of their analysis and the inadequacy of their understanding of both the nature of welfare intervention and the needs of user groups. Seeking to meet the spiritual needs of a diverse group of parishioners, as Ellis has already shown, is a far more complex undertaking than selling socks. Effectiveness cannot be measured by some crass reference to profit margins and turnover.

The training orientation ensures that preparation for welfare work corresponds to perpetually shopping on a limited budget, where the decision is continuously between meat or potatoes. Whatever the choice, all parties remain dissatisfied. Nobody is ever publicly content with professional welfare training. The gaps all seem unbridgeable; the emphasis misplaced; the content inadequate to the needs; and the trainers, like generals, are always accused of fighting the current war with the tactics and weapons of the last. Before readers rush to accuse us of adding to the clamour for the reform of training it is essential to state that we are not advocating reform but root and branch replacement by education.

Such a transformation would entail the construction of a mode and curriculum that sought to develop in practitioners an ability to reflect upon, and make theory, about practice. However, such activity would have to be contextualized, linked to and integrated with the elaboration of a more general philosophical and social analysis. Possessing an understanding of what makes for good in human relationships; a disposition to undertake actions which promote the good rather than the correct; the ability to think critically; a reportoire of images and experiences; and the capacity and commitment to engage in dialogue – these, we argue, are the central requirements for all who wish to engage in socially just welfare work. The problem with skills–led training is that it is incrementally bolted on to a partial analysis of practice and purpose. Faulty and restricted perceptions of essential role, purpose and practice ensure that the skills taught must be inadequate to the task. Sustained analysis and theory making become superfluous within this model, being perceived as 'obscuring reality' and 'getting in the way of action'. In the end, it is only by luck that any contribution to the good can be made. Overwhelmingly, skills–led training obscures the development of understanding about what exists, what is good and what is to be done.

At this juncture a number of questions arise that cannot be ignored. If skills training is so bad, why is it so popular? Why, for example, after a century of teacher training, eighty years of social work and fifty years of youth work training, do the bulk of managers, practitioners, trainees and trainers possess such touching faith in it, holding firm to a belief that with a little more time, a little more effort and a little more cash they will produce a winning formula?

Inevitably no single answer exists to explain so much wasted effort and misplaced faith. Among those that compete for attention the following must be included. Training offers the apparent potential of minimizing overheads: only that knowledge and skill deemed to be self-evidently applicable need be taught or leant. For management this is clearly attractive – a point we will return to. However, it needs to be stressed that the training orientation also appeals to many practitioners and trainees. For a number, training is a purely utilitarian process that provides a conduit to higher status and/or income, entry to a profession or progress up the greasy pole once inducted. Quality of service delivery, let alone improvement in the life chances of the client group, becomes important only insofar as it might enhance their careers. Indeed, social and economic equality, insofar as they erode the differentials acquired as a consequence of training or 'education', need to be opposed or marginalized.

Substantive numbers of students will be as crudely committed as managers to a minimalization of training, be it expressed in terms of time, the range of knowledge to be learnt or the monetary cost. However, given that they are being inducted into a caring, person-centred career, such students must actively seek to obscure their crude affiliation to the utilitarian model. Learning the public persona of the profession will entail for some, possibly many, the marshalling of generous helpings of humbug and cant. Seeing this as an aberration would be simplistically naïve. Rather it should be counted as a key ingredient within their induction. Deceiving the trainers is essential practice for deceiving clients, colleagues, the public and, in some cases, themselves. Given that such a skill is one usually learnt early on in both school and working life only the most 'immature' or incompetent fail in this respect and deservedly so, not least because they, by their very naïvety, stupidity or crass ignorance, would come to threaten the survival of the whole edifice. Demanding skills and training, rather than reflective education, these students, wittingly or unwittingly, make this deception all the easier. For in the end what is assessed is overwhelmingly that which can be most accessible to measurement and testing. Accordingly unless legal standards of competence are demanded, or there exist real risks to the employer of incurring penalties for incompetence, standards, whether of practice or theoretical competence, will remain low, partly because the whole notion of training is predicated on the principle that if the tasks are broken down to their constituent elements, and the instruction programme constructed to meet the 'needs' of the students, then all must graduate. Failure on the part of the student thus becomes transposed into a failure on the part of the tutor or course.

Not surprisingly, a minimalist training model is also appealing to those who, often correctly, assume that they would fail a more demanding and intellectually rigorous programme. In narrowly fixing the parameters of learning, as well as the input, it becomes more feasible to calculate the outcome. Wonderful, except that the outcome is guaranteed to be substantially irrelevant to the real tasks that face practitioners.

Trainers, both within and without the education system, have shown considerable sympathy towards the adoption and development of a skills-led orientation. Educators are as other welfare workers likely to reject those approaches that place a primary emphasis upon the critical and reflective engagement with practice. A number of explanations need to be considered. At a basic level, money talks. Resources are increasingly available for targeted forms of skill training. In the context of welfare, the skills identified are frequently associated with attempts to do something about some current moral panic. Examples are legion: dealing with AIDS; controlling disruptive behaviour; spotting the abused child; handling violence; countering burn-out; managing prejudice. While undoubtedly practitioners may require information in these areas, they hardly constitute a coherent programme for the development of practice or policy. Incremental and pragmatic training of this kind largely operates upon a deficit model of the practitioner, frequently transposing what are failures of policy and structure into the training arena. Rather than throwing money at problems, the tendency is now to throw training. In this way the state or agency demonstrates its concern without necessarily having to do much or threaten entrenched positions.

Another attraction has been that the pedagogic and curricular styles linked to the skills approach appear to offer solutions to a number of long-standing educational problems. At last ways can be found to measure teacher and lecturer input, student outcome, practitioner performance and cost effectiveness, all within the framework of tight behavioural objectives. The skills and talents of the entrepreneur, the Freddie Lakers and Clive Sinclairs, have found a renewed route into education. Beyond the comfort of measurability lies the nirvana of relevance. Instead of grappling with abstract concepts and imponderables, educationalists and students are offered the gratifying prospect of encountering the concrete and the immediate. 'Tricks of the trade' could be learnt in the morning and exercised in the afternoon: doubly exciting and rewarding for all parties when applied to the heady issue of the moment.

Skill-led training provides a ready means of dividing academic labour. Lecturers and tutors can specialize in discrete competences such as counselling, group work, family therapy, prejudice management, time management, stress abatement. As the openings grow, so the list expands. These and others can then be modulized, compartmentalized and packaged ready for consumption. Learning clusters can, with a flick of the Filofax, be painlessly cobbled together. Advocates of the student-centred approach can be assuaged by the provision of a spurious notion of student and/or employer choice. Satisfaction is guaranteed for all parties with options which allow students to avoid difficult, uncomfortable and subversive areas of knowledge. At the same time the growing influence of employer-led curricular design and funding allow the problems to be addressed in a technicist fashion. Structural questions can be side-stepped, the inadequacies of the learners emphasized and the commitment of employers signalled merely via the 'laying on' of a course. All of which neatly reinforces the centrality of management.

The training model neatly dovetails with key managerial assumptions. We can illustrate this in a number of ways. Particular difficulties surround the management of many professional welfare workers. These frequently arise because workers enjoy a relative freedom to organize their own programme and initiate work; their activities can often be undertaken independently of others; and there are considerable physical and occupational obstacles to direct supervision (Smith 1979). In these circumstances training, particularly that provided in-service, becomes an attractive option. Rather than attempting to instruct workers to operate in a particular way or to conform to a particular style, managers can call upon trainers and consultants. Through the medium of training sessions and courses, the desired disposition to exercise certain skills and to operate identified working practices can be inculcated or encourated (Jeffs and Smith 1988: 230–51).

While the contemporary rhetoric of managerialism may laud such characteristics as flexibility and transferable skills, such assertions require careful interrogation. The labour market continues to require workers ready and willing to undertake routinized tasks. Flexibility, therefore, is often directed towards deskilling. For example, the integration of physical with emotional care in the residential setting results not in the elevation of the manual aspects of care but in the routinization of relationships and the marginalization of the theoretical insights that flow from the social sciences. Further, the lower the level of skill required for a job, the easier it is to train someone to undertake such work and the possibilities for more 'flexible' staffing are enhanced. Transferable skills are seen overwhelmingly in horizontal terms. This is not predicated upon a desire to integrate manual and mental labour in order to erode the role of management. Rather the predominant concern is to enhance management. Management, within this enterprise, becomes a transferable skill like other welfare functions. What is important here is that an over-archingly hierarchical delineation is retained; indeed the intention, if not the end result, is that it is strengthened.

Although many 'customers' find the training approach attractive and user-friendly, in the end it is flawed. The reasons for this, we have argued, are varied but fundamental to the enterprise. We therefore wish to argue for an alternative that places critical thinking at its core. Some practitioners, and certainly many employers, will find this uncomfortable. We make no apologies for that. Indeed, if the interests of the client groups are placed at the centre of the welfare enterprise then we have no choice but to begin discomforting substantial numbers of both groupings.

Educating for informal education

It is a well-trodden pathway within the training of welfare workers to teach by doing. Caseworkers are taught casework by being caseworked; teachers by being taught; and group workers via group work. This approach can be extremely restrictive, particularly if insufficient attention is paid to the cognitive and to interrogating practice. There are likewise problems in using informal education in this way. The arguments developed in our opening chapter regarding the limitations of this form of pedagogy should encourage a certain reluctance to proceed along that route. While practitioners will need informal educational experiences, a range of more formal methods will be required in order that the material generated can be reflected upon and theorized (see Chapter 9 in this volume).

In order to explore what some of the key elements of a programme of education for informal educators may be, it is necessary to revisit our understanding of the processes involved. These are set out in Figure 1.1. From this a number of themes are soon apparent.

Approaching cultures

Central to the informal educational process is the ability to develop an appreciation of the cultures encountered and the ways in which interventions may be understood. In particular, practitioners have to make the familiar strange; to stand aside from taken-for-granted assumptions about the ideas and behaviours they encounter within different cultures, including their own. What is of importance here is not prepackaged knowledge about specific cultures, but the enhancement of the general ability to engage with cultures, to learn about them, to recognize the dynamics and tensions within them and to identify appropriate points of intervention. This engagement can easily float free of the circumstances in which it develops. It is thus necessary within educational programmes to explore the ways in which culture is activated by the relations between different classes and groups, bounded by structural forces and material conditions and 'informed by a range of experiences mediated, in part, by the power exercised by a dominant society' (Giroux 1983: 163). In other words, seeking to know what the different cultural forms are and how they are experienced, is not enough. We also have to bring into active consideration the various forces and ideologies which influence people as they make and remake the cultures of which they are a part.

All this provides a considerable agenda for the education of welfare practitioners. Taken as a discrete element, the size of just this educative task might seem huge. For example, students would have to be asked to examine their own biography, cultivate their ability to engage with ethnographic processes and be able to locate this within an understanding of the dynamics of subordination and dominance in society. For many, if not most, such a process would be dependent upon a significant change in their own perspectives and modes of thinking. It is obvious, therefore, that learning about how to approach other cultures cannot be satisfactorily handled within skills-led training. Nor can it be confined to some 'special' module. It can only really be managed in educational situations where people's perspectives, and modes of thinking and acting, are seen as the central and comprehensive problematic, where the concern is to generate critical thinking and to mesh that process with action. When seen in this way, the concern wth culture is an integral part of a complex whole, as indeed is our interest in the other elements that follow. Many of the processes and arenas for reflection, theory making and action thus cut across the traditional competence boundaries.

Informal and everyday social situations

Many practitioners are used to working only in situations where they have a significant degree of control, where the exchanges are fairly formalized or with groups which have a fixed membership. We only have to think of the casework relationship, the therapy group or the classroom to recognize this. The dynamics of the friendship group, the movement and diversity of the youth club, and the discursive nature of 'drop ins', can present the unsuspecting worker with all sorts of difficulties. A significant feature here is the basic level of understanding about informal and everyday social situations. Comprehending the patterns and behaviours that occur in different situations usually takes a considerable amount of time. Approaching the everyday involves a degree of sophistication that is rarely appreciated. It can also involve some role discomfort. Handling anxieties, being able to join in with what is happening and being adept at picking up on alternative routes into situations involves a sizeable investment in reflection and theory making, as well as sustained exposure to appropriate settings. The scale of this task can be easily underestimated, as it frequently entails a major reconceptualization on the part of students. As we will see, it also requires the cultivation of a deep sense of one's own identity as a practitioner.

Developing an understanding of what makes for the good

The question of what makes for human well-being is rarely approached holistically in the training of welfare practitioners. In a number of areas the tendency has been to conceive of this enterprise in almost exclusively psychological terms. In contrast, we see the good as a combination of aesthetic, intellectual and moral meanings which are in a state of movement and formation. Inevitably subjective and personal, such meanings can, nevertheless, be shared with others. As Brown has demonstrated, it is possible to construct a list of basic human goods and to refine them through experience and analysis (1986: 159). While controversy will always surround what constitutes a particular good, or over interpretation, the application of practical reasoning does allow debate and some level of agreement.

Developing and refining understandings of what makes for the good must be a key element in appropriate professional education for this area. Possession of a reasoned sense of what makes for human flourishing, and a commitment to continue to work at such understandings, is essential for emancipatory engagement in welfare. Without it practitioners are at sea. They have only surface considerations upon which to base their decisions and can end up floundering like fish left by the tide or clinging to established procedures and conventions. Developing such an understanding is inevitably complex, drawing upon a range of disciplines and sources. The nature and scale of this investment is made all the more complicated by the fact that what makes for good will alter from situation to situation. It is not something which can be looked up in a handbook and then applied. Rather, practitioners have to engage in a process of continuous reasoning and testing.

Critical thinking

Being a critical thinker:

> involves more than cognitive activities such as logical reasoning or scrutinizing arguments for assertions unsupported by empirical evidence. Thinking critically involves our recognizing the assumptions underlying our beliefs and behaviours. It means we can give justifications for our ideas and actions. Most important, perhaps, it means we try to judge the rationality of these justifications.
>
> Brookfield 1987: 13

While it may be claimed that many courses and training programmes enable their participants to enhance their abilities in this respect, it is only a minority, in our judgement, which provide the context and stimulus that allow such modes of thinking become a lived activity, rather than an 'abstract academic pastime' (*ibid*: 14). That context must include a framework which enables dialogue to take place; the opportunity to engage in the extended study of practice, and the intellectual traditions and material conditions which help shape our understanding of it; and the development of the sort of critical community which allows both theory and practice to be interrogated and related. In this it is necessary to transcend the sharp differentiation between the supposedly particular and everyday sphere of practice and the timeless, universal world of theory. In Chapter 1 we argued for praxis, in which action and thought (or practice and theory) are dialectically related.

> They are to be understood as *mutually constitutive*, as in a process of interaction which is a continual reconstruction of thought and action in the living historical process which evidences itself in every real social situation. Neither thought nor action is pre-eminent.
>
> Carr and Kemmis 1986: 34, emphasis as in original

As Carr and Kemmis go on to argue, in praxis the ideas which guide action are just as subject to change as action is. The only 'fixed' element is the disposition to act for the good, that is to say, to act truly and rightly.

Autonomy and a disposition to the good

Genuinely emancipatory practice embraces a disposition to the good rather than the 'correct'. It embodies a degree of moral consciousness unknown to those concerned with the application of the technical (see Chapter 1). Acting in this way involves positive liberty or authority over one's self (autonomy). That state requires that we have a developed self – the choices made have to be conscious and informed. In addition, it would entail being able to do what we have chosen. Thus, an autonomous person 'has a will of her or his own, and is able to act in pursuit of self-chosen goals' (Lindley 1986: 6).

The process of enabling people to act autonomously is surrounded by rhetoric, particularly in the education and training arena. Talk of the autonomous student, student-centred learning and open learning is difficult to translate into practice, especially when it is adopted by those with a disposition to technical reasoning and to skills-led training. Autonomy is not a thing to be bequeathed by others but is a way of behaving. In that sense it is not something which can be 'taught', though it has to be learnt. As Kitto (1986) has argued, it has to be demonstrated and held within course structures and organization and in the actions of staff. This requires constant vigilance, and a degree of professional openness and cooperation rare within the higher education field. It also involves containing the rescuing instincts of many staff. So-called 'caring' for students can easily increase dependence. Programmes which seriously seek to enhance autonomy will also have to look to making self-assessment the pivot around which other forms of assessment operate. Autonomy 'does not sit easily with the learning objectives approach, which implies a more dependent relationship on the part of the student, with a teacher who knows what should be learnt' (Kitto 1986: 70).

Building a repertoire

Schön (1983: 138) argues that the building up of a repertoire of examples, images, understandings and actions is one of the central ingredients of professional reflection-in-action (emphasis in the original).

> When a practitioner makes sense of a situation he perceives to be unique, he *sees* it *as* something already present in his repertoire. To see *this* site as *that* one is not to subsume the first under a familiar category or rule. It is, rather, to see the unfamiliar, unique situation as both similar to and different from the familiar one, without at first being able to say similar or different with respect to what. The familiar situation functions as a precedent, or a metaphor, or . . . an exemplar for the unfamiliar one.

When thinking about something that has arisen, practitioners may draw on material from widely different contexts. Here, two dimensions are of particular significance – the accessibility of the material and the ability to engage in a dialogue with the situation: experience is only useful insofar as it is accessible. The way in which we organize and think about our experiences is therefore of some importance. Recognizing patterns or retrieving ideas is enhanced by practice and reflection. This process involves practitioners in a dialogue with situations in which they reframe them in relation to what has gone before. These they then test and remake so as to fit more closely the particular. This structure of reflection-in-action requires close attention within the education of welfare professionals. It means that there has to be a substantive emphasis upon enabling practitioners to address their experiences, to think 'metaphorically', to construct and test models and to reframe situations in the light of these activities.

Identity and role

Practice for the good requires deep attention to the way in which practitioners understand and name themselves (Smith 1988: 142–3). In informal education such concern is especially important, given that it frequently forms just one part of practitioners' inventory. For example, social workers have to switch between several roles in the course of a normal working day. At one moment they may be acting as a 'representative of the authority', when exploring a possible example of non-accidental injury; at another they will, perhaps, be counselling an individual who has asked for their services. In between, they could have spent two hours in a drop-in, engaged in informal education. Throughout this process they need to know who they are, what their purpose is and how to employ their thinking and competence in each situation. Crucially, they must have the capacity to switch between the various roles and to communicate this change.

As we saw in the opening chapter, all this cannot be established in isolation. If they are to function effectively, practitioners must have their role accepted by those with whom they wish or need to work. Preparing people for this switching, and enabling them to establish a professional identity which allows them to make sense of the various strands, calls for a high degree of integration and coherence in any educative programme. They are not likely to be well served by off-the-shelf modules. If there are to be various skill specialisms then they must flow out form a firm grasp of the ways in which different modes of thinking and acting interact and connect with, for example, 'the social work task'. That in itself is no mean effort. For, as Howe has argued, the turbulent nature of the social substructure has generated a range of social work, and other welfare, theory (1987: 168). Practitioners have 'to make sense of the whole, dense spread of relationships, some which "blend", some of which "clash"' (*ibid*: 168). Thus, within the education programmes of each of the professional groupings, there has to be an extensive exploration of the nature of the whole and its relationship to its parts. At one level this is obvious; but it is a task from which many in professional welfare training shy away.

Enabling dialogue

We have already dealt with a number of the key dimensions of the process of engaging in dialogue and developing critical thinking. Here the focus is on the educative processes demanded by the task of enabling practitioners to adopt the dispositions, thinking and behaviours associated with critical dialogue. It is our contention that such dialogue should be occurring within professional education programmes if they are fulfilling their promise. Participants should be giving careful attention to words, the ideas they express and the actions that follow. There will be a commitment to collaborative working and to critical engagement with each others' thinking and actions. In this sense college or student sessions can provide a great deal of material for reflection, theory making and action. However, this of itself is not enough. Dialogue should also be manifested in the face-to-face work that practitioners undertake as part of such programmes.

In designing and facilitating programmes that develop and sustain dialogical thinking and action there has been a tendency to focus on method. Small groups are seen as good, lectures are seen as bad. While it may be that a different quality of interaction is possible in the small group, its advancement as the means of enabling dialogue is suspect. What is of central importance is the ethos and direction of the enterprise. Small groups, especially very small groups, can be extraordinarily non-dialogical. The question to be addressed is the extent to which a spirit of critical enquiry is abroad. To what degree are people engaging with ideas and actions and enhancing the discourse? This might be happening in large groups, small groups, pairs or indeed within individuals as they read other's work. What is essential is that the processes and values involved are not overlooked because they are part of the daily round. In other words there should be dialogue about dialogue.

Handling the thinking and action of others

One of the things that practitioners find liberating, and very difficult, about informal education, is the extent to which it calls upon people to take responsibility for their own learning and actions. The process of enabling people to act autonomously can set up a range of frustrations in practitioners. We have to stand by as people decide to go up blind alleys or as things that they organize go 'wrong'. It is all too easy to regress or to import forms of behaviour appropriate to other contexts where it might be our duty to intervene (for example, within certain schooling or social work scenarios). Not only that, the experience can be threatening as demands are placed upon us or as the actions taken might be interpreted by our employers as occurring as a result of our 'leading the group on'. Yet the avoidance of rescuing behaviour and the promotion of autonomous thinking and action, remains central to positive practice.

While there may be workers whose arrogance, paternalism or lack of personal boundaries put them beyond the possibility of development, most have the potential to function as effective informal educators. For this to happen it is necessary to acknowledge feelings and to recognize that at particular moments they can be powerful indicators. Nevertheless, they do have to be channelled. It is here that sustained consideration of what makes for good, an appreciation of identity and role and an ability to think critically are of the utmost importance. Sound analysis and theory can curb rescuing and enable practitioners to function in situations of conflict and apparent uncertainty. However, that analysis does not arise in a vacuum. It is furthered by dialogue and the attempt to construct a critical community among practitioners and others. Where there is praxis, there is possibility.

Evaluating processes and outcomes

Intervention and dialogue produce outcomes in the people directly concerned, others they interact with and the contexts in which they operate. It is an extraordinarily complex matter to unravel just what action has contributed to a specific outcome. Indeed, in many cases it is impossible. Yet evaluation is an integral part of the informal education process. Without it critical practice is unsustainable. At this point, however, it is necessary to place evaluation in context. As Armstrong and Key have demonstrated in respect of community work, evaluation cannot be treated as a neutral technique or method reflecting academic or professional ideas. Rather, it has to be viewed as 'historically rooted in the political economic changes of a develop-ing capitalist society' (1979: 220). More particularly, it must be recognized that much of the growing demand for evaluation arises out of a desire to control rather than learn. It is a means employed by sponsors and managers in order to limit the activities of projects and practitioners.

Within the technical orientation, evaluation is predominantly concerned with the extent to which objectives have been met. In informal education, the interest is in the nature of the processes and in what people are learning. It is not something external to the workers and learners but grows out of the normal work of reflection and theory making. In this sense evaluation cannot be thought of as a one off event, something that is done every so often. Nor is it particularly sensible to hive off the function into a separate role – the evaluator. It is simply part of the process of educating. This has implications for programmes of professional education and brings us back to the necessity for holistic and integrated thinking and prac-tice. Those programmes which actively seek to promote praxis, which endeavour to enable practitioners to engage critically with the world, will consistently require all participants (including staff) to reflect, analyse and judge performance. However, given the em-phasis on product and objective within the dominant training ideol-ogy, considerable attention will have to be given to ways in which understandings of what makes for the good can be applied in the course of learning. Similarly, it will be necessary to cultivate ways of working and thinking which enhance people's ability to make judgements about process.

Conclusion

In this chapter we have only been able to skim across the surface of what education for informal education might look like. It is some-thing which must be integral to programmes of education for the various professional areas. To add it on as some extra module or as an aspect of post-qualifying training simply will not do in the majority of cases. The scale of the task would be as large as that involved in the original initial training. It involves enabling people to behave autonomously, to handle uncertainty and to think. Moreover, it requires overcoming all sorts of bad and lazy practice.

> Many practitioners, locked into a view of themselves as technical experts, find nothing in the world of practice to occasion reflection. They have become too skilful at techniques of selective inattention, junk categories, and situational control, techniques which they use to preserve the constancy of their knowledge-in-practice. For them uncertainty is a threat; its admission is a sign of weakness.
>
> Schön 1983: 69

For the critical informal educator uncertainty is hardly comfortable. However, the nature of the uncertainty they feel is different. Rather than simply being a weakness, it is an opportunity for reflection and action.

Bibliography

Alexander, R. (1988) 'Garden or jungle? Teacher development and informal primary education' in Blyth, A. (ed.) *Informal Primary Education Today: Essays and Studies*. Lewes, Falmer.

Allman, P. (1987) 'Paulo Freire's Education approach: a struggle for meaning' in Allen, G., Bastiani, J., Martin, I. and Richards, K. (eds) *Community Education: An Agenda for Reform*. Milton Keynes, Open University Press.

Allman, P. (1988) 'Gramsci, Freire and Illich: Their contributions to education for socialism' in Lovett, T. (ed.) *Radical Approaches to Adult Education: A Reader*. London, Croom Helm.

Anderson, D. (1982) *Social Work and Mental Handicap*. London, Macmillan.

Armstrong, J. and Key, M. (1979) 'Evaluation, change and community work', *Community Development Journal* Vol. 14, No. 3.

Atkinson, D. (1988) 'Residential care for children and adults with mental handicap' in HMSO, *Residential Care: The Research Reviewed*. London, HMSO.

Baker, J. (1987) *Arguing for Equality*. London, Verso.

Bank-Mikkelsen, N. E. (1976) 'Denmark' in Kugel, R. and Shearer, A. (eds) *Changing Patterns in Residential Services for the Mentally Retarded*. Washington, President's Commission on Mental Retardation.

Barrow, R. (1984) *Giving Teaching Back to the Teachers: A Critical Introduction to Curriculum Theory*. Brighton, Wheatsheaf Books.

Bernstein, B. (1971) *Class Codes and Control*, Vol. 1. London, Routledge & Kegan Paul.

Berry, P. (ed.) (1976) *Language and Communication in the Mentally Handicapped*. London, Arnold.

Blyth, A. (ed.) (1988) *Informal Primary Education Today: Essays and Studies*. Lewes, Falmer.

Booton, F. (ed.) (1985) *Studies in Social Education*, Vol. 1, 1860–1890. Hove, Benfield Press.

Bottoms, A. and McWilliams, E. (1979) 'Non-treatment paradigm for probation practice', *British Journal of Social Work*, Vol. 9, No. 2.

Brew, J. Macalister (1943) *In the Service of Youth*. London, Faber.

Brew, J. Macalister (1946) *Informal Education: Adventures and reflections*. London, Faber.

Brew, J. Macalister (1957) *Youth and Youth Groups*. London, Faber.

Broad, B. (1985) 'Community development in Probation: which way forward?' *Probation Journal*, September.

Brookfield, S. (1983) *Adult Learning, Adult Education and the Community*. Milton Keynes, Open University Press.

Brookfield, S. D. (1986) *Understanding and Facilitating Adult Learning*. Milton Keynes, Open University Press.

Brookfield, S. D. (1987) *Developing Critical Thinkers: Challenging Adults to Explore Alternative Ways of Thinking and Acting*. Milton Keynes, Open University Press.

Brown, Allan (1979) *Groupwork*. London, Heinemann Educational Books.

Brown, Allan (1986) *Modern Political Philosophy: Theories of the Just Society*. Harmondsworth, Penguin.

Brown, R. I. (1977) 'An integrated programme for the mentally handi-capped' in Mittler, P. (ed.) *Research to Practice in Mental Retardation*, Vol. II, *Education and Training*. New York, University Park Press.

Carr, W. and Kemmis, S. (1986) *Becoming Critical: Education. Knowledge and Action Research*. Lewes, Falmer.

Clark, D. (1987) 'The concept of community education' in Allen, G., Bastiani, J., Martin, I. and Richards, K. (eds) *Community Education: An Agenda for Reform*. Milton Keynes, Open University Press.

Clayton, G. (1987) 'Community Education Review: Interim Report'. Leicester, Unpublished report, Leicestershire Education Department.

Coleman, J. S. (1976) 'Differences between experiential and classroom learning' in Keeton, M. T. (ed.) *Experiential Learning*. San Francisco, Jossey-Bass.

Coombs, P. H. and Ahmed, M. (1973) *New Paths to Learning*. New York, UNICEF.

Craft, M. (1979) *Tredgold's Mental Retardation*. London, Bailliere Tindall.

Craven, A. (1968) *West Africans In London*. London, Institute of Race Relations.

Davies, B. (1979) *In Whose Interests? From Social Education to Social and Life Skills Training*. Leicester, National Youth Bureau.

Davies, B. (1986) *Threatening Youth: Towards a National Youth Policy*. Milton Keynes, Open University Press.

Davis, A. (1981) *The Residential Solution*. London, Tavistock.

Dean, A. and Hegarty, S. (eds) (1984) *Learning for Independence*. London, Further Education Unit.

Department of Education and Science (1983) *Young People in the 80s: A Survey*. London, HMSO.

146				*Bibliography*

Department of Education and Science (1985) *Report by HM Inspectors on Westhill College, Selly Oak, Birmingham: Initial Training for Community and Youth Work.* London, DES.

Department of Education and Science (1986) *Report by HM Inspectors on the YMCA National College: 2 Year Certificate Course.* London, DES.

Department of Education and Science (1987a) *Effective Youth Work: A Report by HM Inspectors.* London, DES.

Department of Education and Science (1987b) *Report by HM Inspectors on the Technical and Vocational Education Initiative in South West Leicestershire.* London, DES.

Department of Education and Science (1988a) *Management of Schools: A report to the Department of Education and Science by Coopers and Lybrand.* London, DES.

Department of Education and Science (1988b) *Report by HM Inspectors on University of London Goldsmiths' College Community and Youth Work Course.* London, DES.

DHSS (1988) *Community Care: Agenda for Reform* (The Griffith Report). London, HMSO.

Dewey, J. (1966) *Democracy and Education: An Introduction to the Philosophy of Education.* New York, Free Press.

Dewey, J. (1963) *Experience and Education.* New York, Macmillan.

Donges, G. (1982) *Policy Making for the Mentally Handicapped.* Farnborough, Gower.

Drakeford, M. (1983) 'Probation – containment or liability?', *Probation Journal*, Vol. 30, No. 1.

Feek, W. (1988) *Working Effectively: A Guide to Evaluation Techniques.* London, Bedford Square Press.

Fenn, G. (1976) 'Against verbal enrichment' in Berry, P. (ed) *Language and Communication in the Mentally Handicapped.* London, Arnold.

Fletcher, C. (1987) 'The meaning of "community" in community education' in Allen, G., Bastiani, J., Martin, I. and Richards, K. (eds) *Community Education: An Agenda for Reform.* Milton Keynes, Open University Press.

Fordham, P., Poulton, G. and Randie, L. (1979) *Learning Networks in Adult Education: Non-formal Education on a Housing Estate.* London, Routledge & Kegan Paul.

Foreman, A. (1987) 'Youth workers as Redcoats' in Jeffs, T. and Smith, M. (eds) *Youth Work.* London, Macmillan.

Foreman, K. (1987) 'Lost election blues', *Community Education Network*, Vol. 6, No. 6.

Freire, P. (1972) *Pedagogy of the Oppressed.* Harmondsworth, Penguin.

Freire, P. (1985) *The Politics of Education: Culture, Power and Liberation.* London, Macmillan.

Gardner, J., Murphy, J. and Crawford, N. (1983) *The Skills Analysis Model.* Kidderminster, BIMH.

Gilleard, C. (1984) *Living With Dementia.* London, Croom Helm.

Giroux, H. A. (1983) *Theory and Resistance in Education*. London, Heinemann.

Goffman, E. (1961) *Asylums*. Harmondsworth, Penguin.

Gray, B. and Isaacs, B. (1979) *Care For the Elderly Mentally Infirm*. London, Tavistock.

Griffiths, H. (1982) *Making a Start: A Consultation Document*. Coventry, Working Party on a National Structure for Community Development.

Grundy, S. (1987) *Curriculum: Product or Praxis*. Lewes, Falmer.

Gunzberg, H. (1963) *Progress Assessment Charts*. London, National Association for Mental Health.

Health Education Council (1986) *Who Cares? Information and Support for Carers of Confused People*. London, Health Education Council.

Henderson, P. and Thomas, D. N. (1987) *Skills in Neighbourhood Work*. London, George Allen & Unwin.

HMSO (1960) *The Youth Service in England and Wales* (The Albermarle Report). London, HMSO.

HMSO (1969) *Report of the Committee of Inquiry into Allegations of Ill-treatment of Patients at the Ely Hospital, Cardiff*. London, HMSO.

HMSO (1971a) *Report of the Fairleigh Committee of Inquiry*. London, HMSO.

HMSO (1971b) *Better Services for the Mentally Handicapped*. London, HMSO.

HMSO (1982) *Experience and Participation: Review Group on the Youth Service in England* (The Thompson Report). London, HMSO.

HMSO (1988a) *Residential Care: A Positive Choice. Report of the Independent Review of Residential Care* (The Wagner Report). London, HMSO.

HMSO (1988b) *Residential Care: The Research Reviewed*. London, HMSO.

Howe, D. (1987) *An Introduction to Social Work Theory*. Aldershot, Wildwood House.

Hudson, B. (1984) 'Femininity and adolescence' in McRobbie, A. & Nava, M. (eds) *Gender and Generation*. London, Macmillan.

Hunter, R. and Scheirer, E. A. (1988) *The Organic Curriculum: Organizing for learning 7–12*. Lewes, Falmer.

Illich, I. (1973) *Deschooling Society*. Harmondsworth, Penguin.

Jarvis, P. (1987) *Adult Learning in the Social Context*. London, Croom Helm.

Jeffree, D. and Cheseldine, S. (1982) *Pathways to Independence*. London, Hodder & Stoughton.

Jeffs, T. and Smith, M. (1987) 'What future for initial training?'. *Youth and Policy*, No. 20.

Jeffs, T. and Smith, M. (eds) (1988) *Welfare and Youth Work Practice*. London, Macmillan.

Jeffs, T. and Smith, M. (1989) 'Taking issue with issues', *Youth and Policy*, No. 26.

Jones, C. (1989) 'The end of the road? Issues in social work education' in Carter, P., Jeffs, T. and Smith, M. (eds) *Social Work and Social Welfare Yearbook 1*. Milton Keynes, Open University Press.

Jones, K. (1975) *Opening the Door: A Study of New Policies for the Mentally Handicapped.* London, Routledge & Kegan Paul.

Jones, K. (1989) 'Community care' in Carter, P., Jeffs, T. and Smith, M. *Social Work and Social Welfare Yearbook 1.* Milton Keynes, Open University Press.

Kay, D., Beamish, P. and Roth, M. (1964) 'Old age mental disorders in Newcastle. Part one: A study of prevalence', *British Journal of Psychiatry*, No. 110.

Kelly, A. V. (1982) *The Curriculum: Theory and Practice.* London, Harper & Row.

Kiernan, C. and Jones, M. (1977) *Behaviour Assessment Battery.* Slough, NFER.

King, R. (1988) 'Informality, ideology and infants' schooling' in Blyth, A. (ed.) *Informal Primary Education Today: Essays and studies.* Lewes, Falmer.

Kitto, J. (1986) *Holding the Boundaries: Professional Training of Face to Face Workers at a Distance.* London, YMCA National College.

Kolb, D. (1976) *Learning Style Inventory.* New York, McBer & Co.

Konopka, G. (1963) *Social Group Work: A Helping Process.* Englewood Cliffs, NJ, Prentice-Hall.

Kugel, R. and Shearer, A. (eds) (1976) *Changing Patterns in Residential Services for the Mentally Retarded.* Washington President's Commission on Mental Retardation.

Lewis, J. and Meredith, B. (1988) *Daughters Who Care.* London, Routledge & Kegan Paul.

Levin, E. Sinclair, I. and Garbach, P. (1983) *The Supporters of Confused Elderly Persons At Home.* London, NISW.

Lindley, R. (1986) *Autonomy.* London, Macmillan.

Linge, K. (1986) 'Setting up a relative support group', *Community Care*, October.

Lodge, B. and McReynolds, S. (1983) *Quadruple Suppot For Dementia.* Leicester, Age Concern, Leicestershire.

Lovett, T. (1988) 'Community education and community action' in Lovett, T. (ed.) *Radical Approaches to Adult Education: A Reader.* London, Croom Helm.

Mace, N. and Robins, P. (1985) *The 36 Hour Day: Caring at Home For Confused Elderly People.* London, Hodder & Stoughton.

Martin, I. (1987) 'Community education: towards a theoretical analysis' in Allen, G., Bastiani, J., Martin, I. and Richards, K. (eds) *Community Education: An Agenda for Reform.* Milton Keynes, Open University Press.

Mezirow, J. (1983) 'A critical theory of adult learning and education', in Tight, M. (ed.) *Education for Adults*, Vol. 1, *Adult Learning and Education.* Milton Keynes, Open University Press.

Mittler, P. (1979) 'Training: education and rehabilitation. An overview' in Craft, M. (ed.) *Tredgold's Mental Retardation.* London, Bailliere Tindall.

Mittler, P. (ed.) (1977) *Research to Practice in Mental Retardation*, Vol. II, *Education and Training*. Baltimore, MD, University Park Press.

Morris, P. (1969) *Put Away*. London, Routledge & Kegan Paul.

National Advisory Council for the Youth Service (1987) *Young People, Work and Enterprise*. London, DES.

National Advisory Council for the Youth Service (1988a) *Participation: Part A. Guidelines for Youth Service Policy Makers*. London, DES.

National Advisory Council for the Youth Service (1988b) *Participation: Part B. Guidelines for Youth Service Practitioners*. London, DES.

National Advisory Council for the Youth Service (1988c) *Participation: Part C. Guidelines for Young People*. London, DES.

National Advisory Council for the Youth Service (1988d) *Youth Work in Rural Areas*. London, DES.

National Advisory Council for the Youth Service (1989) *Youth Work with Girls and Young Women*. London, DES.

National Association of Probation Officers (1984/5) *Community Based Practice: A Discussion Document*. London, NAPO.

Necomb, T. (1961) *The Acquaintance Process*. New York, Holt, Rinehart & Winston.

Nias, J. (1988) 'Informal primary education in action: Teachers' accounts' in Blyth, A. (ed.) *Informal Primary Education Today: Essays and studies*. Lewes, Falmer.

NISW (1982) *Social Workers, Their Role and Tasks* (The Barclay Report). London, Bedford Square Press.

Northamptonshire County Council (1987) *14–16 Curriculum Report: Annual Report 1986–7*. Northampton, NCC.

Papwell, C. P. and Rothman, B. (1966) 'Social groupwork models: possession and heritage', *Journal for Education for Social Work*, Vol. 2, No. 2.

Rawlings, C. and Peacock, B. (1986) 'It's nice that someone takes an interest in me', *Community Care*, 9 January.

Richards, R. (1986) 'Control not choice', *Community Education Network*, Vol. 6, No. 9.

Robb, B. (1967) *Sans Everything*. London, Nelson.

Rosen, A. (1972) *Residential Provision for Mentally Handicapped Adults*. London, Tavistock.

Rosseter, B. (1987) 'Youth workers as educators' in Jeffs, T. and Smith, M. (eds) *Youth Work*. London, Macmillan.

Russell, B. (1971) *Principles of Social Reconstruction*. London, Unwin.

Russell, M. G. (1983) 'Black-eyed blues connections' in Bunch, C. and Pollock, A. (eds) *Learning Our Way*. London, Crossing Press.

Schön, D. A. (1983) *The Reflective Practioner: How Professionals Think in Action*. London, Temple Smith.

Scottish Education Department (1987) *HM Inspection of Schools: Aberdeen College of Education, Aberdeen*. Edinburgh, Scottish Education Department.

Shearer, A. (1981) *Disability: Whose Handicap?* Oxford, Blackwell.

Smith, G. (1979) *Social Work and the Sociology of Organisations*. London, Routledge & Kegan Paul.

Smith, M. (1982) *Creators not Consumers: Rediscovering Social Education*, Leicester, National Association of Youth Clubs.

Smith, M. (1988) *Developing Youth Work: Informal Education, Mutual Aid and Popular Practice*. Milton Keynes, Open University Press.

Stenhouse, L. (1975) *An Introduction to Curriculum Research and Development*. London, Heinemann.

Stern, V. (1987) 'Crime Prevention – the inter-organizational approach' in Harding, J. (ed.) *Probation and the Community: A Practice and Policy Reader*. London, Tavistock.

Stone, C. (1987) 'Youth workers as caretakers' in Jeffs, T. and Smith, M. (eds) *Youth Work*. London, Macmillan.

Thomas, D. N. (1983) *The Making of Community Work*. London, George Allen & Unwin.

Thomas, E. J. (1967) 'Themes as in small group theory' in Thomas, E. J. (ed.) *Behavioural Science for Social Workers*. New York, The Free Press.

Thomas, H. (1985) 'Schooling and the maximization of welfare' in Ribbins, P. (ed.) *Schooling and Welfare*. Lewes, Falmer.

Toogood, P. (1980) 'Tomorrow's community education' in Fletcher, C. and Thompson, N. T. (eds) *Issues in Community Education*. Lewes, Falmer.

Townsend, P. (1962) *The Last Refuge*. London, Routledge & Kegan Paul.

Ungerson, C. (1987) *Policy is Personal: Sex, Gender and Informal Care*. London, Tavistock.

Webb, I. (1987) *People Who Care: A Report on Care and Provision in England and Wales*, London: Cooperative Women's Guild.

Welton, J. (1985) 'Schools and a multi-professional approach to welfare' in Ribbins, P. (ed.) *Schooling and Welfare*. Lewes, Falmer.

Whelan, E. (1984) 'The Copewell Curriculum: development, content and use' in Dean, A. and Hegarty, S. (eds) *Learning for Independence*. London, Further Education Unit.

Woods, S. and Shears, B. (1986) *Teaching Children with Severe Learning Difficulties: A radical reappraisal*. London, Croom Helm.

Wright, F. (1986) *Left To Care Alone*. Aldershot, Gower.

Index

interactionalist perspective, 76
and neighbourhood, 83–4
process, 3, 4, 7, 15–16, 17–19, 20,
58, 72, 87, 117–21 *passim*, 126,
141–2
product, 7, 15–16, 20, 72, 87, 126,
141–2
professional education and
training, 43, 65, 113–23 *passim*,
124–43 *passim*
professional identity, 12–13,
19–23, 73, 139–40
profiling, 63, 71
programmes, 15, 17, 25, 84–7
purpose, 7, 15–16, 17–19, 35

Rawlings, C., 107
records of achievement, 71
reflection-in-action, 19, 138–9
repertoire, 18, 138–9
residential work, 1, 8, 22, 133
and custodianship and control,
37–8
and education, 38, 39
and informal education, 41–6
skill acquisition, 38
status, 46–8
task, 37
respect for persons, 10
Richards, R., 69
Robb, B., 101
Robins, P., 102
role and identity, 19–23, 51–3,
139–40
Rosen, A., 43
Rosseter, B., 27
Russell, M. G., 57

Saddington, D., 1–23 *passim*
Scheirer, E. A., 6, 16
Schön, D. A., 138, 143
schooling, 1
African and Afro-Caribbean
experience, 113–16
extra-curricular activities, 62,
63, 67

and informal education, 4–5,
5–6, 22, 61–74
schools' councils, 62
and youth work, 50–1, 62, 65
Scouts, The, 27
self-assessment, 63, 138
self-management, 22–3, 50
settings, 3–4, 6–7, 26
Shearer, A., 43
Shears, B., 40
Sinclair, E. A., 1–23 *passim*, 134
Sinclair, I., 100
skills-led training, 128–34
Smith, G., 22, 133
Smith, M., 4, 6, 11, 13, 15, 103,
129, 133, 139
social education, 1, 25, 26, 53,
65
social group work, 81–2
social interaction, 3
social and life skills, 26, 33, 38
social service departments, 100
social work, 19–20, 21, 27, 139–40
and education, 39, 103–5,
106–12
and group work, 106–11
special and severe learning
difficulties, 36–48 *passim*, 62
Stenhouse, L., 15
Stern, V., 75
Stone, C., 35
story-telling, 2, 59, 91
supervision, 119
switching, 14, 20, 21, 139

teachers, 20–1, 51, 61–74
Technical and Vocational
Education Initiative (TVEI),
62, 66–7, 70, 74
technological rationality, 40, 138,
142
theory and meaning making, 10,
12, 15–16
Thomas, D. N., 87, 127
Thomas, E. J., 81
Thomas, H., 61